STATE STREET

STATE STREET

One Brick at a Time

ROBERT P. LEDERMANN

Charleston   London

THE
History
PRESS

A cobblestone brick from State and Washington Streets found in front of Marshall Field's, July 15, 1978. This was one of the original bricks off State Street that was dug up from the street. These bricks were lying about when the bulldozers ripped up the street to make new pavement for the State Street Mall. *Photo © Robert P. Ledermann.*

Published by The History Press
Charleston, SC 29403
www.historypress.net

Front cover: Photo courtesy of the *Chicago Sun Times* Newspaper Media/Archival Department.
Back cover: Courtesy of the *Chicago Sun Times* Newspaper Media/Archival Department.
Postcard from Robert P. Ledermann's private collection.

First published 2011

Manufactured in the United States

ISBN 978.1.60949.294.6

Library of Congress Cataloging-in-Publication Data

Ledermann, Robert P.
State Street : one brick at a time / Robert P. Ledermann.
p. cm.
Includes bibliographical references.
ISBN 978-1-60949-294-6
1. State Street (Chicago, Ill.)--History. 2. Chicago (Ill.)--History. 3. Chicago (Ill.)--Biography.
4. Chicago (Ill.)--Social life and customs. 5. Chicago (Ill.)--Economic conditions. 6.
Shopping--Illinois--Chicago--History. 7. Department stores--Illinois--Chicago--History. 8.
Field, Marshall, 1834-1906. 9. Marshall Field's (Department store) I. Title.
F548.67.S73L44 2011977.3'11--dc23
2011028001

To my loving and wonderful wife, Annette M. Ledermann,
for her tireless hours of help and patience in helping me in completing this, my third, book.
And to three especially great children who love to read: Kaitlyn, Julia and Ryan.

CONTENTS

PREFACE

Writing a book was an adventure. To begin with it was a toy, an amusement; then it became a mistress, and then a master, and then a tyrant.
—Winston Churchill, London, November 2, 1949

Churchill's quote, I believe, relates directly to and is a clear description of literally anything that needs to be done correctly. These words require thought. They apply to my newest book on Chicago's State Street and some of its history and happenings. Every book needs to have a beginning, middle and end. In this book, I want to convey some of the exciting research and knowledge I found.

State Street—its history and future—will follow within the chapters and pages of this book and will conclude with a glimpse of how the street is today. My original thoughts of writing go back as far as the 1980s. I always wanted to write about State Street and its people, who made and left their marks. I personally worked with many people who had dealings with the numerous stores up and down the street. Throughout my working career in retail and the credit field, I have met mentors who all encouraged me to write about one of my passions: Chicago's State Street. My membership in and friendship with the Illinois Retail Merchants Association and the Chicago Loop Alliance (formerly the Greater State Street Council) have supported me, and I value the times in my life I spent with them.

My love and interest in Chicago's history is shared by my wife, Annette. Together, we have collected an extensive amount of historical memorabilia and continue to seek out "special finds" from time to time.

My previous writing includes my two books *Christmas on State Street: The 1940s and Beyond* and *Chicago's State Street Christmas Parade*; articles in the *Chicago Historical*

Society Magazine, Antiques and Collecting Magazine and *Nostalgia Digest Magazine*; and a 2010 calendar.

One would think, perhaps, that there would be no Chicago history had it not been for a fur trader and frontiersman named Jean Baptiste Point Du Sable. His wife, Catherine, a Pottawatomie Indian, settled in the area near the shore of the Chicago River. He built and developed a living complex consisting of a farm, a trading post and a five-room home (at that time considered a mansion), complete with a long, covered porch to overlook the river. He was an Afro-French trader who forged up and down the Illinois River between Michigan City and Peoria, Illinois, in the late 1770s. Du Sable was highly respected by Native Americans and other traders. He sold his holdings and home to John Kinzie to move his family to what was then the Spanish Upper Louisiana Territory, today's St. Charles, Missouri. Du Sable's fur trading was becoming a more limited enterprise. International businessman John Jacob Astor of New York started the American Fur Trading Company and soon monopolized the Great Lakes fur trading area.

John Kinzie was born in Quebec in 1763 and moved to Detroit, Michigan, before settling into the Du Sable homestead. He was also adapted to the land and made his fortune with the surrounding trading communities.

Social life was kept to a minimum. People woke at sunrise, only to fill their days with good old-fashioned self-reliance. The basic life skills for self-sufficiency were the definitive activities of each day. Filling the oil lamps, feeding the livestock, cleaning the barn, making soaps, washing and sewing clothes and cooking meals were all women's duties. There was perhaps an occasional church function to break up the mundane life. Usually, only men stopped in at the few "taverns" that dotted the area while they were trapping or trading to have a simple meal or strong drink, attend to the needs of their horses or rent a bed to rest the night, all the while talking and making deals with other traders.

The Chicago area was being recognized as "The Place" for retail, architecture, financial investment and growth, one brick at a time.

ACKNOWLEDGEMENTS

It is my sincere pleasure to thank these especially wonderful people without whose knowledge, friendship, support and understanding this book could not have been written. I will never forget them. I truly appreciated these fine people and the extraordinary photos and information they provided. Thanks to:

Ben Gibson, commissioning editor at The History Press, who was integral in producing this book. His help was most appreciated. Without Ben, there would be no book!

Mary L. Holmstrom, licensing coordinator at the *Chicago Sun-Times*, and publisher John Barron, who said, "YES."

Russell Lewis, executive vice-president and chief historian of the Chicago History Museum. He should be commended for his diligence in seeing that the History Museum pictures in this book were graciously released.

Stephanie Zimmermann, *Sun-Times* "Help Line," who opened the legal doors for me.

Jon Jones, Macy's Inc./visual director State Street, who was outstanding in his support and release of several important photos and information captured in his book. He is keeping the magic alive, and it's wonderful!

Lydia Brown, who was extremely helpful and supportive in this venture, as well as in other projects. She is a wonderful asset to Macy's.

Ward Miller of the Richard Nickels Committee, Chicago, who has been remarkable not only in his knowledge of Sullivan Center (formerly Carson, Pirie, Scott) but also in allowing me to publish for the first time in any book the photos of the mysterious Carson's Clocks.

Blair Kamin of the *Chicago Tribune* newspaper.

Margaret Cimoli, a real great lady who shared with me her experience and photos of her time in the Walnut Room Restaurant at Marshall Field's (now Macy's).

ACKNOWLEDGEMENTS

Laura Jones and Ty Tabing, executive director of the Chicago Loop Alliance (formerly the Greater State Street Council). These fine people have always supported me in my research on Chicago.

Mary Wolf of Old St. Mary's Church on 1500 South Michigan Avenue.

Jack Shimmerling, a gifted artist who was gracious enough to allow me to put two of his fantastic watercolor paintings of State Street into this book.

And last but not least, Jerome and Jennifer Smith, who gave of their time freely for several months, compiling the words of my book onto the computer. They are truly a special asset to anyone who knows them. Their help will always be remembered.

One brick at a time...

1

STATE STREET

The Beginnings

The military reservation of Fort Dearborn was built and established at the eastern edge of the settlement, defined by Dearborn Street and the river. It was under the command of Captain John Whistler, grandfather of the famous artist James A. McNeill Whistler. The fort itself was rebuilt in 1816 after the Indian uprising, with the settlers housed there. Fort Dearborn was named for Henry Dearborn, secretary of war.

The houses and small buildings near the fort were constructed mainly out of wood from the northern woods with logs of strong timbers. They were certainly not an imposing sight, but they were warm and served the residents with shelter from the severe winter weather. The roofs were simple thatched bark on thin wooden shingles. Every home was heated by a fireplace that doubled as the cooking area. They first buried their dead right next to their houses, which accounts for the occasional skeleton bones unearthed during the construction of newer buildings near the area of the riverbank at Lake Street.

The city of Chicago was incorporated on March 4, 1837, and started out simply with a filthy, muddy, dusty strip of muck called State Road. State Road went westward and took travelers from Chicago to the present-day towns of Rockford, Elgin and Galena, Illinois. Galena was a thriving mid-sized city, while parts of Chicago were still unpaved village. The name State Street grew out of that road—a "State Road" between Vincennes, Indiana, and Chicago. It was later known as "Old State Road," and then in 1833, the Chicago section became our State Street. The name stuck.

State Street existed with wooden planks as sidewalks. Chicago's population was approximately 4,170, yet its residents still had no gas to light or heat their homes, no paved streets and no buildings taller than two stories.

The first Fort Dearborn, 1803–12. The first Fort Dearborn was built and commanded by Captain John Whistler and stood on what is now the southwest corner of Michigan Avenue and Wacker Drive. It was made of logs, as was the Agency House on the riverfront. The Agency House was used for trading with the Indians and was burned on the day after the Dearborn Massacre, August 16, 1812, at the same time as the first Fort Dearborn. *Courtesy of the Chicago History Museum* (ICHi-59714).

A group of five trustees was elected to adopt a municipal code. The first ordinance was to establish the town's limits: Ohio Street on the north; Jackson Street on the south; Jefferson and Clark Streets on the west; and on the east, the lake as far as the river and south of that, State Street.

Within three years, on March 4, 1837, a city charter was incorporated and adopted by the legislature that made Chicago a city. Six aldermen were elected and served without salaries. Mayor Ogden received $500 a year for his services.

John Kinzie lost the race to be the first mayor of Chicago to William B. Ogden, although he would later become president of the Chicago Historical Society (now the Chicago History Museum), founded in 1847. Back on State Street, men, women and children had to wear high-topped, buttoned shoes or boots as they dodged mud holes and horse-drawn carriages and pushcarts that splashed them constantly with mud.

It's interesting to note that some of the first commercial dealings on State Street were those of the water merchants who sold Lake Michigan water to nearby residents of the city because few of the water wells were uncontaminated. Later, Chicago's first municipally owned pumping engine was Old Sally, a steam-powered, single-action pump of eight-million-gallons-per-day capacity. Its pumping station was linked to a tunnel two thousand miles long under Lake Michigan, providing water to Chicago. This was in 1857–58. Old Sally was in continuous use for years at the Chicago Avenue pumping station, until it was replaced by a more modern engine.

Across the street, the Chicago Water Tower has been one of our city's cherished landmarks. Designed in 1867 by architect William W. Boyington, it stands tall today as a memorial to the victims of the Great Chicago Fire and as a symbol of the indestructible will of a city to endure.

The basic atmosphere was still dirty and grimy, but the growth of the city was bustling, even though the Chicago River continued to overflow its banks, slopping thick mud along Lake Street's main business and shopping area. Women would cover their noses with perfume-drenched handkerchiefs to mask the terrible smell of the horses, raw sewage and mud. The main retail dry goods store at Lake

The seal of the City of Chicago, 1833–1905. This is a reproduction of what, for many years, was the official seal of the City of Chicago. Made of marble, thirty-two inches in diameter, it adorned one of the interior walls of the old city hall, razed in 1908. The seal was preserved and, in 1954, presented to the Chicago Historical Society, now known as the Chicago History Museum. *Courtesy of the Chicago History Museum.*

Street, south between Clark and LaSalle, was Potter Palmer's shop, considered to be the top of its field in those early days.

Even before Chicago was incorporated as a city, one of the first established commercial businesses was the grocery and liquor store of Stiles and Burtons at the corner of State and Lake Streets, across from St. Mary's Catholic Church. Both the store and the church were built in 1833–34. This was the very first Roman Catholic church in the city, designed and built by Augustine Deodat Taylor, showcasing his new "balloon-frame" architecture style in a wooden building that was less costly to complete. St. Mary's was the first church to have a grammar school.

In 1843, the Dioceses of Chicago was established, and it was decided to build a new church at Madison and Wabash Avenues, closer to its parishioners and nearer to State Street, leaving the "old" church to be sadly destroyed by the fire of 1871. St. Mary's was relocated five times before it finally acquired its last permanent location at 1500 South Michigan Avenue, with its teachers and school building at 1532 South Michigan. It stands today with a proud corner stone plaque that reads:

Old St. Mary Church
The Paulist Fathers
Dedicated July 21, 2002
Francis Cardinal George
Founded 1833
Chicago's First and oldest Parrish

This is not to be confused with the oldest Catholic building: Old St. Patrick's Church at 140 South DesPlaines Street. It was constructed between 1852 and 1856, making it the oldest church still existing at its original location, on its original construction structure. It was one of a slim group of historical buildings that did not perish in the Great Chicago Fire of 1871. It survived with relatively little damage and finally became a designated historical landmark in 1964. It proudly boasts one of Chicago's most beautiful collections of stained-glass windows.

Life in Chicago was exciting and filled with surprises, there was no question about that. The businesses were doing as well as expected. History, as they say, was in the making. The School of the Art Institute opened in 1866.

Potter Palmer came from Albany, New York, to Chicago in 1852 to make his fortune in the dry goods business. He was born on May 26, 1826, the fourth of seven children. When he was twenty-six, he left his small dry goods store in Lockport, New York. It wasn't proving the success he had hoped, and he thought a bigger metropolitan area would perhaps suit his liking. At that time, Potter Palmer hired no women but

The first house in Chicago was on the north bank of the Chicago River, just south of the present site of the *Chicago Tribune* offices. It was built by Jean Baptiste Point Du Sable, a San Domingoan, in 1784. Du Sable later sold the home to a French trader, Le Mai, who in 1804 sold it to John Kinzie. *Courtesy of the Chicago History Museum* (ICHi-01222).

instead catered to their needs. At his store, the sign "P. Palmer Dry Goods & Carpets" hung over the door. This dominated Lake Street in the 1860s. Palmer would later be known as the first merchant prince of State Street. His original dry goods store was the catalyst for other notable men who would be connected with State Street, men like Montgomery Ward, Levi Leiter and Marshall Field. Palmer gave all these men an education and training in detail in all aspects of the retail business. He advertised in the newspaper *Journal* about his store as the "Cheapest Place in Town." It's interesting that all four men had their starts in small dry goods businesses, and all had a passion to continue on that path to become successful.

Potter Palmer married his bride, Bertha Honore, in 1870 and started a family. Mrs. Palmer was a remarkable woman. She was born into a Louisville, Kentucky aristocratic family that had relocated to Chicago. She was twenty-one, well educated,

The Chicago Ship and Sanitary Canal of January 11, 1900. The waters began to trickle through as the last lock was opened. According to Lloyd Lewis and Henry Justin Smith in *Chicago: The History of Its Reputation*, "Downtown crowds stood on the bridges…to watch the unfolding miracle of a brown old river, turned blue; to see if it performed the impossible, and slide away from the lake." The Chicago River had reversed its flow. *Courtesy of the Chicago History Museum.*

beautiful and known for her gowns and diamonds. Palmer, who was forty-four when he married Bertha, offered as a wedding gift the first Palmer House Hotel, nearing completion. Two sons—Honore and Potter Palmer II—were born. With his family growing and his wife known as the queen of Chicago's high society, Palmer purchased inexpensive parcels of swampland northward on what is known today as Michigan Avenue and on Lake Shore Drive. In the Gothic early Romanesque style, he built an enormous mansion nicknamed "The Castle." The architects were Henry Ives Cobb and Charles Summer Frost. Construction started in 1882 and was completed in 1885.

To say the residence at 1350 North Lake Shore Drive received all the bells and whistles was an understatement. It had a separate interior architect: Joseph Lyman

Silsbee. The Palmers enjoyed buying works of art and paintings for their Castle even more when Bertha was named chairwoman of the Colombian Exposition's Board of Lady Managers. The art gallery in the Palmer mansion included paintings by Charles Monet, Pierre-Auguste Renoir and Edgar Degas. Later, these paintings were donated to the Art Institute of Chicago. A strange, little-known fact, perhaps, is that their mansion's outside doors had no door knobs. The only way to be admitted from the outside was to be acknowledged by a servant, who escorted you in. The butler would take your calling card and place it on a small silver tray, and then the parlor maid would present it to the Palmers for approval. Sadly, this fantastic home was demolished in 1950 for the development of a twenty-two-story high-rise apartment building.

To answer the need for a place where Chicago businessmen could spend their leisure time, entertain or have meetings, social clubs were established. Both the Chicago Club and the Standard Club were founded in 1869. These clubs were strictly dominated by males. They had many rules and regulations upon which the members agreed. These clubs were for the elite, wealthy and educated businessmen who would one day become the political and civic-minded leaders of Chicago. After the fire in 1871, one of the first women's club was the Fortnightly, founded in 1873. It basically started out as a private girls' school to help teach young women literacy and the social graces of the day. It is one of the few women's organizations that still remains today, with its main purpose of promoting the arts and keeping the club a mainstay of Chicago's social society. Mrs. Bertha Palmer became a member in 1880.

As far as Palmer was concerned, his Lake Street store had served its purpose. There were greater opportunities for growth and development on State Street, formerly named old State Road. With his own wealth and financial backing, he purchased land parcels and slowly began acquiring properties on State Street. By 1867, he had acquired about three-fourths of a mile along State Street and had $600,000 worth of construction projects underway. One of his concerns was a new store—a six-story building at the corner of State and Washington Streets constructed from limestone and marble. The newspapers dubbed it the "Marble Palace."

Levi Leiter was born in 1834 in Leitersburg, in Washington County, Maryland, founded by his grandfather. As a child, he also worked for a dry goods company in Springfield, Ohio. He married Mary Theresa Carver in 1866. Going into partnership with Marshall Field and Palmer, Leiter was on his way in the retail business. On the Marble Palace's opening day, the men received cigars, and the ladies were presented with roses. This completely new and fresh concept was most welcome, and the store again catered to the female sex. Women and housewives appreciated the new and pleasant way to shop.

Young Marshall Field's bride at that time, Nannie Scott, gave a few of her own ideas in the planning stages of the Marble Palace, suggesting wider aisles to accommodate all the fabric of women's long dresses and a place to sit down to relax with a cup of tea. Women were getting more interested in the styles and fashions from New York and Europe. They now wanted imported Italian silks and materials, fine furniture, china, rugs and such to make their homes more refined and elegant. This new store was the fabulous retail endeavor that Field and his two partners had been looking for. They were independent and financially successful.

Potter Palmer's health was failing, and he was growing tired of the dry goods business. He decided to go into semiretirement, although he kept the lease on the State Street store. He continued with his real passion: overseeing his properties and construction interests. One such property was the original eight-story, 225-room Palmer House Hotel at the corner of State and Monroe Streets. He enjoyed his real estate developments to the fullest, as any businessman would. The land boom was thriving on State Street. Values rose from $500 a foot in 1860 to $2,000 a foot in 1869.

Then, on October 8, 1871, Chicago was enjoying a warm and hot Sunday. Almost no rain had fallen for three months. The trees had already lost their leaves, and the water wells were dry. They say the fire alarms were slow, and by the time the first fire engines arrived, the flames had spread to nearby dry buildings. In an incredibly short time, the fire was out of control. The flames ate through the wooden structures in their path. The businesses on State Street were destroyed. The fire took from both the wealthy and the poor. Potter Palmer lost the store, the hotel and other properties along State Street. Fortunately for Palmer, he was able to borrow $1.7 million on his "personal character" to rebuild State Street. It was written that this amount of money was the single highest amount ever loaned to an individual at one time. (In addition to the economic depression that Chicago experienced in 1857, Chicago had to deal with the Civil War from 1860 to 1865. Horrific as the war was, the perk to Chicago was that the Union forces closed down the Mississippi River during the war, choking off all river trade down to St. Louis, the older and largest rival city to Chicago.)

After the devastation of the fire, the re-growth of the city was swift. It forced the money changers, engineers, designers, businessmen, architects and manufacturers to all come to do their part. Chicago wanted and needed to heal quickly. Relief came into Chicago from all over the country and from abroad. President Ulysses S. Grant sent $1,000 to the relief committee. Even books, totaling over eight thousand, were donated by private concerned persons from England, including Alfred Lord Tennyson, Robert Browning, Benjamin Disraeli and Queen Victoria. The Chicago Water Tower on Michigan Avenue was used as a temporary library.

Police Department, early 1900s. Chicago's city charter of 1837 provided the city with its first police force—one constable for each of the six wards acting under a higher constable. Here, policemen line up for the inspection of uniforms in the 1900s, all with the high quality of the profession that was the standard of the force. *Courtesy of the Chicago History Museum.*

The population grew from 298,977 in 1870 to 1,700,000 by 1900. Horsecars up and down State Street were replaced with cable cars in 1882. Some of the first railroads were completed, all radiating out of Chicago. The Galena & Chicago Union, the Michigan Central, the Michigan Southern and the Illinois Central tracks all ran parallel to the river, connecting with canal barges filled with lumber, grain and supplies that could easily be transferred into lake ships. The Outer

Above: Vintage postcard, turn-of-the-century view of the main aisle, first floor (nearly four hundred feet long) of the Marshall Field store. *Robert P. Ledermann, private collection.*

Opposite: Cover of the Marshal Field and Co. children's *Juvenile World Magazine*, October 1921. This was a publication for boys and girls and their parents. This issue concerned the story of the Great Chicago Fire, which left our city in ashes. But it explains to the children that from the ashes Chicago began to build anew and has become the great city it is today. *Robert P. Ledermann, private collection.*

Belt Line Railroad accommodated travel and the transfer of needed goods to the nearby towns of Aurora, Joliet and Elgin. The surrounding wheat and grain farms thanked Cyrus H. McCormick for inventing his grain reaper, enabling the farmers to harvest their fields sooner and faster. Chicago had established itself as one of the fastest grain exchanges, with grain elevators dotting the landscapes.

The agricultural and lumber industries were also in demand. Lumber as a commodity and for raw metals sprouted sawmills to manufacture lumber for more farms, homes, buildings and fences. The distilling and brewing companies got a foothold in Chicago, too. U.S. South Works had huge demands for its iron and steel. R.R. Donnelly & Sons had the printing field covered. Hart, Schaffner & Marx started their vast garment company. The list goes on and on with names like International Harvester and Pullman; and lets not forget Midwest dairy and livestock, with meatpackers Philip D. Armour and Gustovus Swift.

In Upton Sinclair's famous book *The Jungle*, printed in 1906, he exposed the substandard activities and the poor quality of processing meat in the Chicago Stock Yards. This brought about federal food inspections and laws—the rules and regulations that mandate the standard of meat goods today.

With its impressive crowds of people from all walks of life, shopping began and continued on State Street. This driving force was the meager start of the soon-to-be Chicago retail empire, despite all the obstacles that stood in its way.

One brick at a time…

2

MR. MARSHALL FIELD

As the story goes, on September 18, 1834, Marshall Field was born the third child to father John and mother Fidelia Nash. He had two older brothers, Chandler and Joseph. His younger brother was Henry, and his two sisters were Helen and Laura. It's not clear how many other siblings died in childhood. His father and mother had a two-hundred-acre farm in the Berkshire Hills, just about a mile from Conway, Massachusetts.

His parents instilled in all their children a strong work ethic. Even before school started, young Marshall Field would wake up early every morning to do his farm chores. The farm stood on what was known as "Field's Hill." It had an especially beautiful view, overlooking the wide valley of the Connecticut River, at an elevation of more than one thousand feet. Marshall Field, in his later life, was accustomed to say about his homeland, "One might travel far over the world and see nothing finer." This quote was taken from a special book printed in remembrance of the dedication of the library Marshall Field built for his parents and the town of Conway. This library and the book—and how important they were to Field—will be discussed later in this chapter.

In his younger years, Marshall was content and quiet. In the peaceful surroundings, his twelve-hour days were filled with farm life, church and school. He had few friends and kept mostly to himself. The few school chums he did count on gave him the nickname "Silent Marsh." After his graduation in 1851, the young and imaginative Field, at seventeen, left his pastoral existence to seek out employment in a small dry goods store in the nearby town of Pittsfield, Massachusetts, where he stayed for five years and learned the tricks of the trade. He was a fast learner and, at twenty-two, had had enough of small-town living. Field headed west to Chicago. He obtained

Mr. Marshall Field. *Robert P. Ledermann, private collection.*

employment as a clerk with the firm Cooley, Wadsworth and Company, a wholesale and dry goods house at 205 South Water Street. The next year, 1857, the firm moved to a new location on Wabash Avenue between Benton Place and Lake Street and changed its name to Cooley, Farwell and Company. By 1860, Marshall Field had become a successful manager in the firm and had gained much respect; he became a full partner in 1862.

As a young man with a bright future and financial backing, Marshall started to attend social activities outside the world of business. He accepted invitations to parties and social events. It was at one of these parties that he met his bride-to-be, Nannie Douglass Scott. Marshall was twenty-eight, and she was twenty-three. Nannie had all the polish, grace and beauty of any debutante of the day, acquired at the notable Miss Willard's School for Young Ladies in Troy, New York. She was a delicate young woman who definitely turned young Field's head. It was said that Field was so impressed with Nannie at first sight that when she took the train back home to Irontown, Ohio, young Field ran after her train, jumped on board, introduced himself again and told her of his affection and feeling for her. They were married in her hometown in 1863 and returned to Chicago to start a new life together. They had three children. Their first baby, Lewis, was born in 1866 but sadly passed away before his first birthday. Shortly thereafter, Marshall Field II, known as "Junior," was born in 1868, and their only daughter, Ethel, followed in 1873.

As the children were growing, the Fields' marriage was interrupted and became more and more compromised. Marshall would plunge himself into his business, and the store's concerns were his first priority. He had little time left in his days for hearth and home. Nannie frequently took Junior and Ethel to Europe because she and her husband were constantly quarreling. She was unhappy with the social pressure of competing with the likes of Bertha Palmer, the queen of Chicago's social life. Spending more and more time traveling, Nannie Field preferred the higher lifestyle in the popular cities of Europe. They had all the traditional standards of culture that she, and especially her daughter Ethel, enjoyed. She refused to jockey back and forth in Chicago's social circle. She decided to leave that to the two biggest "high-society" grande dames: Edith Rockefeller McCormick and Bertha Palmer.

It seems these ladies were always trying to out do each other. Who would make the bigger arrival at the Opera House's opening night? Who would have her own plum-colored Rolls-Royce with her private chauffer dressed in a matching plum-colored uniform drive up to the doorway? Any time dear Edith told the press that she and her party would be attending the opening night of the opera, it became a guarantee that it would be a sold-out performance. But then, Edith had no comparison to Bertha's famous New Years parties. It was the invitation that everyone waited to receive. It was a who's who event that would indicate who would be noticed and invited to all the year's activities and parties of the elite in Chicago. Bertha Palmer really outdid herself when she held the wedding and reception of her sister, Ida, who was marrying none other than the eligible bachelor Frederick Dent Grant, the handsome son of President and Mrs. Grant. All of Bertha Palmer's parties were predictable: they were the very best of the best, with no exceptions.

Nannie Field remained in Europe traveling and spending time enjoying all the riches of her lifestyle. Ethel Field spent most of her young life in Europe. She later advised her parents that she would be permanently moving to England to be married. She married within her social rank to Admiral David Beatty, First Earl of Beatty, making Edith the Countess Beatty. She and the admiral had two sons: David Field Beatty, who became the Second Earl of Beatty at his birth, and Peter Randolph Louis Beatty. Ethel passed away in July 1932 and was buried in Dingley, Leicestershire, England.

At home, Marshall Field also elected to spend money, but in different ways. He became a true friend to Chicago, donating $1 million to help establish the Field Museum of Natural History, with an additional $8 million to be given after his death. He donated ten acres of land he owned to start building the University of Chicago and was one of the founders of the Art Institute of Chicago. He believed that along with power and financial success comes a sense of public responsibility. The Chicago Art Institute was originally part of the Columbian Exposition and was called the Academy of Fine Arts.

Marshall Field's sister-in-law was married to his younger brother, Henry, who came to Chicago in 1861 and was known for his humanitarian efforts and love for the arts. He was a member of the Chicago Relief and Aid Society and one of the first members of the board of trustees of the Art Institute of Chicago. After his death, as a memorial tribute to Henry, his widow commissioned sculptor Edward L. Kemeys to create the two lions that flank the outside of the Chicago Art Institute. They were unveiled in May 1894. The south lion "stands in an attitude of defiance." The north lion is "on the prowl."

Back in the city, the firm changed its name to Farwell, Field and Company. Marshall's friend and acquaintance, Levi Z. Leiter, was a bookkeeper and credit man. Together, they created a partnership with Potter Palmer to establish the new Field, Palmer and Leiter Store on October 12, 1868. They asked the city council to broaden the width of the street to copy the likes of Parisian-style boulevards. With resolve, some of the neighbors refused to set their buildings back to accommodate them. New rules of retailing allowed goods to be returned for an exchange or full cash refunds. Sending goods on approval and bargains were also new ideas. Success was everywhere; Chicago was on its way.

In 1867, Potter Palmer gave control of his business to Field and Leiter but remained their landlord. Eventually, he sold all his shares to them. Things were going well, and Field made a neat $12 million the first year. They established the first foreign affairs office in Manchester, England. The business was flourishing—until the Great Chicago Fire of 1871 destroyed Chicago. Field, Leiter and Palmer were devastated but determined to rebuild. They returned to State Street and Washington in 1873 with a new five-story building. This was short-lived, as another fire, this time within the store itself, caused extensive damage. The store was redecorated, repairs were made and it finally reopened in 1879.

Along with the store, Field owned a massive interest in Chicago's coal and steel industries. Chicago was becoming a booming metropolis. The city's population grew. The railroad, livestock, grain, trade and lumber industries all flourished after the fire, and so did Field. In 1881, Leiter retired. Marshall Field bought out Leiter's share and renamed the store on State Street "Marshall Field & Company." He now arrived at the store at about 5:00 a.m. and allocated work to his head department managers like a sergeant in the army. He told them to teach his employees to be pleasant at all times to the customers. The famous quote "Give the lady what she wants" was his final remark following a conflict between a clerk and a lady customer.

Field gave strict orders for the care of his horses. In my opinion, he must have had a great love and endearing appreciation for horses. According to the book *Give the Lady What She Wants*, "It is indicated that Marshall Field said, 'If any driver brought back a horse with whip marks, they would be severely reprimanded and often be discharged.'" On the walls of the horse barns were constant reminders that the animals were to be treated well. One sign read, "Don't whip the horses," and another, titled "The Horse's Appeal to His Master," pleaded, "Of water stint me not, of whips task me not, and don't forget to blanket me."

Few people would see this softer side of Field. Most people saw only the stern, cold, steel-blue eyes and a face that seldom smiled. Self-made, he fought every obstacle that came his way. Sadly, during the Haymarket Riots of 1886, he was asked his opinion

The handwritten letter from July 1899, on Marshall Field's personal stationery, to Robert Todd Lincoln, acting president of the Pullman Railroad Company. He was asking for a favor for his stenographer Mrs. Chamber's transportation to the state of Washington. *Robert P. Ledermann, private collection.*

of the labor leaders who tried to organize a labor union. Field recommended, "Shoot to kill." He fought hard against labor unions but treated all his employees as though they were unionized. An attempt to organize the drivers to strike against the store was quickly quelled with the establishment of the new Illinois State Board of Certification. If the stock boys didn't come to work with a coat or mittens, he gave them coats and mittens. Another time, he called on his friend in the railroad business, Robert Todd Lincoln, to help arrange—all at Field's expense—for a sleeping car and round-trip transportation for his office stenographer and her sick son, who needed to see a special doctor in another city.

As a side note, if you're interested in knowing about Robert Todd Lincoln, he was the only child of President Abraham and Mary Todd Lincoln to survive to adulthood. He was serving under General Ulysses S. Grant in the Union army when his father was assassinated in 1865. Later, after the Civil War ended, he was a successful lawyer and businessman as chairman of the Pullman Railroad Company. He fell in love with the town of Manchester, Vermont, and in 1905 built a mansion in the Georgian Revival style on 412 acres of land he called Hildene. He and his family spent summers there until his death in 1926. The estate passed down through the family until 1975, when his granddaughter left it to the Church of Christ, Scientist. This twenty-two room mansion is open for tours today.

In 1890, Marshall Field was declared to be the richest and most powerful businessman in the city. But his personal burden grew greater when he learned that his wife, Nannie, died in the South of France in 1896. She was brought back to Chicago and was buried in the Field family plot in Graceland Cemetery at Clark and Irving Park Road.

Postcard of the interior of the Field Memorial Library, Conway, Massachusetts. The white cloth–covered book entitled *The Field Memorial Library, Conway, Mass.*, was printed by Reverend Charles B. Rice in 1907 for one of the family. This book commemorates the services at the laying of the corner stone on July 4, 1900, and at the dedication and opening of the building on July 13, 1901. It belonged to Marshall Field's nephew, Stanley Field. *Robert P. Ledermann, private collection.*

It is interesting to note that the Field crest of 1868 was on the delivery trucks, shopping bags, uniforms, gift tags, elevator doors, paper bags, escalators, etc. The chevron, with its three sheaves of wheat, dates back to thirteenth-century England and was adopted for use in the store six centuries later. The original was sable and black, which represented the character of the first bearer and meant stability and diplomacy. The roof-like chevron meant protection, and the sheaves of wheat meant wealth and prosperity. Wheat was the chief production of the family. The silver of the sheaves of wheat meant that the wealth was the reward of upright dealings. The upper half contained two shocks of wheat, representing a field—hence the Field family. Those two shocks stood for the two older brothers, Chandler and Joseph. The lower shock of wheat represented Mr. Field. The Field's motto was *Sans Dieu, Rien*, or "Without God, Nothing."

In 1899, feeling nostalgic for his hometown and wanting to do something tremendous as a tribute to his mother and father, Field went home to Conway to choose a site to build the Field Memorial Library as a gift for the people of Conway, Massachusetts. Planning this library to honor his parents engaged Field in much joy, and doing this was one of his greatest pleasures. The exterior was of limestone construction with a copper dome. The interior, with an impressive rotunda, is solid marble of various colors. Portraits of his mother and father are in the North Reading Room. In this memorial to the trustees of the library, Field provided a free service for the people in the town, along with a financial endowment for the library's upkeep and for any improvements that might be necessary in the future. Since then, a new roof, a fire alarm system, handicapped accessibility, new lights and beautifications of the landscape have been added. And today, the memorial library is still open, modernized with videos, a bookmobile, Internet access and reading programs for young people.

They say the library's dedication was one of the most memorable public events in the history of the town of Conway, Massachusetts. Fancy invitations were sent to all residents and nearby librarians, and Conway's collection of local dignitaries came to see and hear Marshall Field. Although he was not much of a speaker, his heart was true and filled with pride and joy when he gave the dedication speech:

> *I am exceedingly grateful to see so many of the citizens of Conway here to take part in the dedication of this building. It is now fifty years since I left you, but I have never lost interest in the town or its inhabitants. It is now my privilege and great pleasure to present this token of my friendship, as I do, in memory of Father and Mother, and to you, Mr. Hunt, in behalf of the Trustees, I deliver the deed of the property and the endowment fund and the keys with the hope that the library will give pleasure to all the inhabitants of Conway, that will be a power for good and a lasting benefit to this community.*

Above the entrance are the words "Free to All" and the inscribed names of the citizens of Conway who lost their lives in the Civil War. This information was taken from the book written about the event, edited by the Reverend Charles B. Rice, pastor of the Church of Congregationalists in the Conway area.

Field found himself growing sad and lonely living at his Prairie Avenue mansion. He felt alone, even though the home was filled upstairs and downstairs by domestic servants, gardeners, coachmen, doormen, cooks, butlers and maids. Field had hired Richard Morris Hunt, the preeminent American architect, to build his home. Hunt also designed the base pedestal of the Statue of Liberty and Cornelius Vanderbilt's mansion, The Breakers, in Newport, Rhode Island. Each main room of Field's mansion contained a fireplace, where house maids continued to maintain the fires throughout Chicago's winters. There were huge, thick velvet drapes that hung from

An elaborate circa 1900 horse-drawn parcel wagon that Marshall Field used to deliver packages to his customers. Not many were constructed. *Courtesy of Macy's, Inc.*

floor to ceiling in deeply recessed windows to limit the cold drafts that blew off Lake Michigan to the east of Prairie Avenue. His mansion was one of the first homes to have electric wiring. The rooms not being used for the day had sliding or pocket doors that were richly carved or inlaid with veneers and were closed off from the rest of the house. Some rooms had burled walnut paneling with parquet flooring. The elegant main entranceway, parlor and free-standing staircase all had elaborate wood with ornate carvings. Black walnut and oak wood were hand rubbed to attain a satin finish.

Mr. Marshall Field

Chicago's three wealthiest citizens, all living on Prairie Avenue in 1877, were Phillip D. Armour, George M. Pullman and Marshall Field. Other strong Chicago families like Kellogg, Studebaker, Otis, Glessner, Kimball, Allerton, Streeter, Logan and Bartlett lived at some time on Prairie Avenue. Usually, these mansions were solid brick construction with rock-faced brick or stone façades detailed with various styles of architecture, including French, Gothic Revival or perhaps Romanesque. Some had mansard roofs, gables, elaborate rooflines with copper trim and gutters. Porticos, ballrooms, music rooms, conservatories, libraries, sitting rooms, billiard rooms—anything, really—were taken into consideration in the construction to make these homes as comfortable as possible.

A major contributor to the construction companies was Jacob Henry's limestone quarry in Joliet, Illinois. He had his own immense mansion built there in 1873. It is still there, standing in all its glory. Naturally, every mansion had its own separate coach house near the back of the property to accommodate all the equipment and carriages and to house the horses. It was said that Marshall Field would wake early every morning and be driven in his carriage to State Street. He would be let off one block away from the store to get some exercise and to keep an eye on his competitors. Marshall Field had many wealthy friends and neighbors, including Arthur and Delia Caton, who lived directly behind the Field mansion on the next block, Calumet Avenue. It, too, had its share of wealthy Chicago citizens: the Goodriches, the Drakes, the Buckinghams and Otto Young. At 2107 Calumet was the Arthur B. Merkers family. In his book *Prairie Avenue*, Merkers chronicles what happens to a family in one of the Prairie Avenue mansions. It's an account of a wealthy Chicago family from 1880 to 1918. It's a good read.

This pocket area of Calumet and Prairie Avenue was known as "Millionaire's Row."

Through the years, since 1857, whenever Chicagoans have desired the finest in dairy products they have chosen Wanzer.

Some of Sidney Wanzer's original stops at the glorious mansions of old Prairie Avenue included the homes of George W. Pullman, Marshall Field, P. D. Armour and Martin Ryerson.

Just as through the years discriminating visitors to Chicago have chosen The La Salle Hotel.

SIDNEY WANZER & SONS, INC.

Wanzer on milk is like sterling on silver

A Sidney Wanzer & Sons, Inc., milk ad, indicating that discriminating Chicagoans, as well as visitors to the La Salle Hotel, selected Wanzer milk products. *Robert P. Ledermann, private collection.*

The grandeur of the architecture of these mansions was extraordinary, reflecting the accomplishments of the owners' particular business successes. All of these mansions had head housekeepers, with various butlers, parlor maids, kitchen help and doormen. The servants had somewhat of a "network" among themselves. Most of them were from Europe and would be "sponsored" by the family by whom they were employed. They were immigrants who were happy at the opportunity to come to America and Chicago. A cook or chambermaid, perhaps, might have a cousin in Ireland or England needing a job and sponsorship. The servants lived very comfortably, making contributions to Chicago's growth and at the same time keeping their integrity.

The neighborhood became the center of social and cultural life, with dinners and lavish balls that were regularly reported in the society pages. Field's son, Marshall II (Junior), married, graduated from Harvard and gave his father much-welcomed happiness with the birth of his first grandson, Marshall Field III. They visited him with less frequency than Field would have liked, even though they were living in the mansion next door on Prairie Avenue.

Field's interests began to change, and he became friendly with his widowed neighbor, Delia Caton. She was Miss Delia Spencer, the daughter of one of the partners in Chicago's important hardware firm Hibbard, Spencer, Bartlett and Company. It's interesting to note that the Chicago Fire of 1871 destroyed the second Hibbard and Spencer Hardware store. William Hibbard kept the temporary business going out of his home at 1701 Prairie Avenue, and his huge home was opened to needy families to shelter and protect them during those terrible early days after the fire. Adolphus Clay Bartlett became a partner in the firm in 1882. He had started as a young janitor with the firm in 1864. In 1930, Hibbard, Spencer, Bartlett and Company celebrated its seventy-fifth anniversary. The "True Value" brand was introduced in 1932.

Delia Spenser married Arthur Caton, who was very much her senior. They had no children. He was wealthy—the owner of all the telegraph lines in Iowa and Illinois. After his death, Delia and Marshall Field became very close and went out socially to various places. Field was becoming serious and asked Delia to accompany him on a trip to England, despite rumors about them back in Chicago. The rumor was that they were more than just friends and neighbors, and perhaps there was a secret tunnel that connected Delia's home to Field's. I'd like to believe his strong Presbyterian upbringing and personal ethics kept Field on the straight and narrow, and perhaps the rumors were just that. They were in love and enjoyed traveling in Field's private Pullman coach back and forth to New York.

Field and Delia took the train to the New York docks and boarded one of the White Star Ocean liners, the *Baltic*, occupying his exclusive set of staterooms on the voyage to Europe. They were married in 1905 at St. Margaret Church in Westminster, England.

Mr. Marshall Field's portrait and private "strong box," used in his State Street store office. *Photo © Robert P. Ledermann.*

Field was happy once again and showered his new bride with jewelry, more travel, music and anything to comfort and spoil her. Life was good to Marshall Field—he and the new Mrs. Field were inseparable. That was to be short-lived.

On November 22, 1905, a short two months or so after his father's remarriage, a shot was heard in the mansion of Marshall Field Jr. He lingered near death in Mercy Hospital for five days while his father rushed back from a New York trip, only to learn that nothing could be done to help his only son. Rumors and gossip about Junior's death followed in the newspapers. What was the real cause of the gunshot? Marshall Field accepted the shooting as an accident. The funeral was private. With his only son gone, who would carry on the Marshall Field name? Field was deep in depression over his only son's death. Delia and his close friends encouraged him to play a bit of golf; perhaps hitting the red golf balls on the white snow might do him some good.

The Chicago Golf Club of Wheaton was a private club. It is the oldest eighteen-hole course in North America and was one of the oldest golf clubs founded by the United States Golf Association in 1894. The foursome that played included Field; President Lincoln's son, Robert Todd Lincoln; Field's nephew, Stanley Field; and Field's long and trusted friend James Simpson, who had started working for Field as an office boy. Marshall Field had respected Simpson's work and loyalty and promoted him to his private secretary.

Despite the development of a sore throat and a nagging cough, Field still traveled with Delia back to New York on business dealings. He became so ill upon arrival that the couple went straight to the Holland House Hotel, where Field was confined to bed rest. By the time Dr. Frank Billings was sent for at the famous Billings Hospital of Chicago to attend to Field, he had developed pneumonia, with a temperature of 107 degrees. He soon slipped away from his dear Delia.

Marshall Field died on January 6, 1906, and Chicago was shaken by the news. Marshall Field's store was closed out of respect for days. His body was sent back to

Chicago for a funeral befitting a head of state at the First Presbyterian Church on South Michigan Avenue. Burial was in Graceland Cemetery in the Field plot, Lot 5, Ridgeland Section, near his beloved son and next to his first wife, Nannie. The Chicago Board of Trade closed in the afternoon, and the street vendors sold black and purple mourning ribbons with Field's picture on them. All of Field's employees packed the Auditorium Theater at Congress and Michigan Avenues for a special memorial service. Every store and shop along State Street was closed in respect. Ten days after Field's death, on January 16, 1906, John G. Shedd became the president of Marshall Field & Company, and both the store and story continue—one brick at a time. One brick at a time…

3

MARSHALL FIELD'S STATE STREET STORE

John G. Shedd became president of the store after Marshall Field's death. He worked for Field as his wholesale manager and was a quick learner. He was promoted from within and rose through the ranks. His sales origins, like Field's, were in the small town of Rutland, Vermont, in rugged New England. He came to Chicago in 1872 with a hefty $300 in his pocket. At his interview with Field for the job, he was quoted as saying, "Sir, I can sell anything," and he proved it. In the first year, he sold $10,000 worth of merchandise and found his salary increased from $14 to $17 a week. He then showed Field that after his first year, he had managed to acquire an additional $260, by banking $5 a week. Field was impressed; he had the special gift of knowing the "characteristics of a man." By 1893, Shedd had been welcomed into partnership with Marshall Field.

Harry Gordon Selfridge was a loyal employee and had the nickname of "Mile-a-Minute Harry." He was one of "the boys" Marshall Field handpicked to be important managers. He was asked to do—and did—almost anything that was needed, but he was unhappy and wanted to go higher up the corporate ladder. After twenty-five years, he was still convinced that Marshall Field had elected to promote and recognize John Shedd over him. He was compensated for his shares in the company's stockholdings and left the store to purchase the Schlesinger and Mayer store. This wasn't to be a business success, and Selfridge was looking to sell out within a short few months of opening the new store. The twist comes into play when the man he thought was his rival turned out to be a good friend. John Shedd helped him sell the property to a group of men named Carson, Pirie and Scott—at quite a large profit to boot. Selfridge was finally content after moving to London, where he started another department store. He became the first merchant of Great Britain until his death in 1947.

Before Field's death, plans were discussed to modify his will to give larger donations to charitable institutions and museums, as well as to rebuild the State and Washington Street store into a much larger complex that would encompass an entire city block: State, Randolph, Wabash and Washington. This main section of the new store was called the "Cathedral of Stores," according to the newspapers. On opening day, over eight thousand customers came to look and shop. This store had so many new things—including the new fleet of seventy-six elevators, various restaurants, a bargain basement and the fantastic Tiffany Dome overhead—that it was truly different from other department stores. It was reported that John Shedd said, "If you cannot find it at Field's, you won't find it anywhere."

The following poem was written by Irving Clay Lambert—since 1892, a twenty-seven-year employee of Marshall Field's—as an expression of the ideals that actuate Field's organization:

"Cathedral of All the Stores"

Untrammeled and fair like a thing of dreams,
its granite walls uprise;
Four square to the world, symmetrical, true,
Its tow'rs neath bending skies.
To the north and south, to the east and west,
Swing gates to wondrous floors.
Building for service, aye, proudly it stands,
Cathedral of all the stores.

And radiant stretch the passes within,
Like fairied aisles they run
Mid postured columns, uplifted and white
Ever and ever press myriad fleet,
Expectant through the doors
Building for service, securely it stands,
Cathedral of all the stores.

Looking down at Field's main aisle, after-hours, circa 1940s. *Courtesy of Macy's, Inc.*

And here ingathered from places anear,
And lands beyond the sea,
Are wonderful waves for uses of men,
Rare works of artistry.
And so shall it stand with a fame unmatched
Here, or on distant shores,
Building for service, the marvel of men
Cathedral of all the stores.

The main entrance on State Street, with its giant monolith columns, is made of the strongest granite. The columns are forty-eight feet, nine inches in height and three feet, six inches in diameter. These pillars were installed as the building itself was being constructed and developed in 1902. They have adorned the entrance since, and it has been said that they are the highest monoliths in the world, excepting those in the Egyptian Temple of Karnack.

The first clock was installed on November 26, 1897, at the corners of State and Washington Streets, and ten years later, in 1907, a second identical clock was installed at State and Randolph Streets. The clocks were designed by Pierce Anderson of Anderson, Probst and White, architects for the State Street store. Each arm frame that supports these clocks weighs seven and three-quarters tons of cast bronze. The clocks are seventeen and a half feet above the sidewalk. The minute hand is twenty-seven inches long, and the hour hand is twenty and a half inches long. The face is forty-six inches across and is made of glass. It is illuminated by lights within the clock, which also keep the clockworks warm and dry. The hands are made of wood. How many times have you said, "I'll meet you under the Field's clock"? This might have been confusing; one might answer back, "Which one?" On November 3, 1945, the *Saturday Evening Post* cover featured Norman Rockwell's famous painting of a clock mender setting the handwork clock at State and Randolph Streets by his own pocket watch. This lifelike original painting can be seen at the Chicago History Museum.

In 1991, the open-space "Aire Atrium" was under construction with a fountain at the base. This area of the building was called Holden Court. It was separated on the ground floor by a loading dock and the alley and on the upper floors by a series of stairwells and firewalls prior to 1991.

The landmark addition of the atrium brought more openness, light and shopping convenience into the center of the store, while preserving the integrity and grandeur of the original building. On the main floor today, there stands the last fountain across from the information bureau.

The original plans of the State Street building designed by architect Daniel Burnham called for a fountain—a place where shoppers could meet, much like the Field's clocks. However, along the way, plans for the fountain were lost. That is, until the architectural firm of Hambrecht Terrell took over the job. They spent hundreds of hours researching the restorative renovation, during which time a drawing of the fountain was discovered. The firm had a fountain built to the likeness and scale of the original plans.

The number of Field's employees varied from 9,000 to 13,800, according to the season. Employees answered and assisted customers at the information bureau. They had a bank of telephone booths and a telegraph and cable service. A travel bureau helped plan trips and provided train and steamship schedules; theater tickets could also be placed on reserve. The postage and lost-and-found sections were kept busy. Information given out by Field's employees was believed to be factual and true, provided in a pleasant and efficient tone of speech. Hardly remembered was the

A street view of Marshall Field's on State and Washington. This is a print of a watercolor painting by artist Jack Simmerling entitled *Holiday Memories on State Street*, 1998. The trumpets and wreaths were a traditional part of Field's decorations. *Print used with permission of John J. (Jack) Simmerling/The Heritage Gallery, Ltd.*

Marshall Field's information bureau, offering stations for the post office, theater ticket sales, information and an "in-house" telephone. Field's allowed guests to send and receive telegrams, consult railroad timetables, use the long-distance telephone and leave messages for friends. Above the service counter was an immense clock, called the "around-the-world clock," with a face displaying a dozen international time zones plus the local hour. *Courtesy of Macy's, Inc.*

knitting studio where free instructions on knitting and other home crafts were given. Field's prided itself on its free gift-wrapping service, using the well-remembered tissue, gold tags, carding and strong gift boxes.

The incredible mosaic Tiffany Dome has about 1,600,000 pieces of iridescent glass, the finest example of its kind in the world. It took fifty artisans a year and a half to install. At the time of the dome's commissioning, John Shedd, the founder of Chicago's famous Shedd Aquarium, helped Louis Comfort Tiffany with every phase, from planning and curving the multicolored fragile glass structures through to its completion. It became a highlight of the vast main floor. The dome was unveiled to the public on September 30, 1907, the first day of the formal opening of the completed retail store. Please note, however, that in 1914, the north Wabash Avenue building was added, completing the existing structure. With this final addition joining the already established complex, it became the largest department store in Chicago, competing with the likes of Philadelphia's John Wanamaker & Co. and New York's R.H. Macy's & Co. Marshall Field's store had come a long way since its temporary location in an old railroad car barn on Twentieth and State Streets after the fire of 1871.

Shedd concentrated on the manufacturing operations and acquired thirty textile mills in North Carolina and Virginia that produced and supplied the stores with fine sheets, towels, linens, bedspreads, blankets, etc., under the "Field Crest" label. This "top label" became a mainstay to anyone who cared about a top-quality line of bed or table linens. Naturally one's initials could be embroidered onto them for a small additional charge. From these mills came other widely diversified products, including drapery fabrics, rugs, floor coverings, curtains, silk, wool, cotton dress fabrics, wash dresses, gloves and other women's accessories. Rigid checks and high standards were ensured by the newly developed Quality Control Bureau in every step of manufacturing.

Services and various departments with colorful and fascinating displays all encouraged the sophisticated or casual shopper to take a look and perhaps make a purchase. The courteous sales staff welcomed the clientele with the etiquette a "Field's" salesperson was expected to have. Strict instruction classes were the standard for the clerks, doorman or floorwalkers.

The selection of special departments was almost endless. In the men's department, for example, one could buy a hand-tailored suit or hand-printed (within the store) personal stationery. There was fine and costume jewelry, ladies' handbags, luggage, gloves, hosiery, perfumes, cosmetics and accessories—all to delight female shoppers. Another first was the wedding bureau, designed to offer anything a bride would ever need. The bridal registry was a must. The large selection at the fashion center was appealing to every type of woman, be she junior, college girl, petite miss, prospective bride, housewife, model or matron. Whatever the shopping seeker came to find, whether for that special occasion or everyday wear, it was all at Field's.

The men's store was the place to purchase a suit of clothes if you valued the best quality for your dollars. The store for men was in the "annex building" at the southwest corner of Wabash Avenue and Washington Street. The store for men occupied six floors and one of the three basements of the building. Here was apparel and accessories for men in a neat, masculine setting quite its own. It was a perfect place for men to

Above: Window display, circa 1930s, complete with a top hat, white ties and tails. *Courtesy of Macy's, Inc.*

Opposite: In the lower second basement, the Pneumatic Tube Room from 1947 monitored and counted all the sales, cash and charge slips and kept a record of each department throughout the Marshall Field's store on State Street. Air through the tubes would make the canisters travel back and forth, up and down the miles of tubing. *Courtesy of* Chicago Sun-Times *Newspaper Media/Archival Department.*

shop and for women to shop for men—"one-stop shopping" in today's words. You could have literally picked up the right fishing tackle for an outdoorsmen and your formal wedding attire—and anything in between—all in one place. Any alterations needed were made by in-house tailors, and the finished product was steam-pressed. If any buttons were lost over the next years, they would be replaced at no charge.

There was a unique restaurant in the annex building of the store for men called the Men's Grill. It had a dome-like ceiling and center fountain that was also designed by Louis C. Tiffany. This multicolored glass dome with its prism lights had ornamental forms of the zodiac signs within each of the twelve mosaic ovals that encircled the

Marshall Field's first automatic elevator, November 1, 1955. Mrs. Robert Albiez had the distinction of being the first customer in Marshall Field's men's store (located at the corner of Wabash and Washington Streets) to push a floor button as Mr. Walker White of Westinghouse, Harold Nutting and Charles Mercer, store manager, looked on. *Courtesy of* Chicago Sun-Times *Newspaper Media/ Archival Department.*

ceiling. This restaurant was discrete and was mostly frequented by businessmen. There was a tobacco shop in the lobby of the men's annex that featured fine "house" and imported cigars. Sadly, it's just a memory now.

The public had opportunity to meet favorite authors in the marvelous book department on the third floor. Browsing the distinguished rare and leather-bound classics was encouraged.

With the European Offices opened, Karastan and oriental rugs were readily available from exotic places like Morocco and Hindustan.

The entrance to the fur storage vaults was like a huge refrigerator door, with the temperature inside near freezing. It was cold enough to rejuvenate the furs and to ensure absolute protection. It had a capacity to house forty thousand furs if needed. It was written that if the coats were placed end to end, the racks would stretch three and a half miles long. But before being stored, every fur piece spent

The book department and, to the right, the rare book section. *Courtesy of Macy's, Inc.*

ninety minutes in the Guardlite chamber, a method of absolutely destroying all forms of insect life.

The china department had the biggest names in fine china—Wedgwood, Royal Doulton, Spode, Minton, Lenox, Copeland and on and on—all competing for shoppers' attention with beautiful displays of each pattern. Brides enjoyed selecting and registering for their favorite china patterns.

Still other specialty departments and shops peppered the store. Field's was well known for the very best tradesman, repairing or servicing nearly anything requested. Meticulous care was given to engravings, silversmith pieces, cameras, clocks, custom-made draperies, window treatments, upholstering—whatever the order called for.

The furniture department was composed of sections with fine imported contemporary, classic, modern or antique furniture. Chippendale, Sheraton and Hepplewhite were all there. It offered beds, lamps, kitchen appliances, housewares, porch and garden items, sports equipment, paper and party favors, as well as a complete cleaning service with house-brand cleaning supplies for sale.

An antique section had crystal, jade, ivories, fine pottery and china figurines, as well as expensive replicas from Alva Studios.

The personal shopping bureau helped female executives and businessmen with their shopping needs when their time was short. Selections were made on their behalf.

The Field's Afar/Gift Court had an array of unique and curiously different, one-of-a-kind gifts: European items from around the world, art wear, Rookwood pottery, decorative pieces of porcelain and marble sculptures. It was truly the place to shop for the "person who has everything." You might find an elegant Burmese carved wooden monkey one day and a brass English doorknocker the next. One year, some of Mary Pickford's (a silent movie star) estate items were sold. In 1986, I can remember the spectacular Eagle and the Crown celebration, promoting all things English, with woolens, whiskeys, fabrics, china and more. For the ribbon-cutting, Field's invited Prince Charles to officiate the opening, along with Lord Wedgwood and Sir Cedric Dickens, the great-grandson of Charles Dickens.

The picture gallery had beautiful paintings, old prints, etchings and a lovely repair service. Your selections could be costume framed along with your photograph, or you could have your portrait taken.

Field himself first went to France to buy Paris bonnets and personally directed their shipment to Chicago so that the ladies of the city might receive them in their original hatboxes.

Field's first permanent office was opened in Manchester, England, in 1871. There were other offices in Belfast, Ireland, and even in Shanghai and the Philippines. Back then, these remote areas of the world had unique merchandise possibilities. Hidden treasures found their way by the swiftest transportation into the various departments of Marshall Field & Company, Chicago, exclusively to the store's specifications. Field was able to import the finest fabrics and articles that could not be obtained in domestic markets.

When it came to women needing employment, it was a serious deal among the store's managers. Women in general wanted to improve themselves with education

This photo, circa 1944, is of a World War II barrage balloon hung in the north light well in Field's, located at Randolph and State Street, that was used to detect low-flying enemy activity. It encouraged the customers to visit the Victory Center, sponsored by the Army Corps of Engineers. *Courtesy of Macy's/Hedrich Blessing Studio.*

and to have the financial opportunities men had. These young ladies had minds of their own. The city was opening up to the popularity of apartments, rental flats and boardinghouses, all suitable for the single female. It was accepted that women who didn't go to college after high school would live at home with their parents, siblings, aunts, single uncles or grandparents until they married. To move to the city and live alone or with a roommate, or in a women's hotel, and be independent was quite the thing for the up-and-coming young woman.

Prior to the invention of the brazier in 1913, women wore corsets, called "undergarments" or "unmentionables." These required special measurements to be taken by female attendants. Usually, lady clerks were kept in the bridal and trousseau, infant wear, women's clothing, china and glassware, lingerie and special "French dressmaking" and formal gown departments. They also were experts on helping their customers in the huge pattern, sewing and fabric department.

Field's kept the male and female employee rest areas separate. Women had their own toilets and coat and locker rooms. As additional care and protection for the female employees, they were permitted to leave the building thirty minutes earlier than the men every day.

By 1880, the store had a solid six hundred female employees in its workforce earning an average of eight dollars a week. The dress code required dark colors, with navy blue preferred, though the occasional white blouse with a navy blue skirt was accepted. The men in sales were expected to wear dark suits they could purchase at a large discount through the store.

Behind the scenes were ample rooms for the welfare and convenience of the employees. There was a lunchroom where all employees could purchase meals "at cost"—pennies on the dollar. There were reading and literary rooms and a medical office to dispense various first aid or medications as needed.

As an employer, Field's had several activities for employees to participate in. One such "outside" activity was the choral music group. On June 5, 1906, the Marshall Field & Company Choral Society gave its first concert in Orchestra Hall. All of the 185 members in this first group were employees of the store. William B. Towsley was organizer, founder and president. Thomas A. Pape was conductor, and Katherine Howard Ward was the accompanist. Mr. Pape, who was conductor from 1906 to 1927, was succeeded by Dr. Edgar A. Nelson, who served from 1927 to 1948. The Choral Society was recognized as one of the finest groups of its kind and was one of

Armistice Day 1918. Marshall Field's main aisle, supporting and praising our military forces at the end of World War I. *Courtesy of Macy's, Inc.*

the oldest industrial choral societies, lasting well over fifty years. Through the years, the tradition of giving two major presentations a year was most welcomed. The spring concert was given each May in Orchestra Hall on Michigan Avenue, and in December, Handel's "Messiah," in an abridged form, was sung in the store's Walnut Room for the Christmas holidays. A rare find today is the long-playing record—called *Marshall Field Choral Society Sings* souvenir album—celebrating the golden (1906–56) anniversary of the music group.

The first floor had massive display cases, with beveled glass surrounding each counter, showing the fine merchandise in that area. Behind each counter, the clerks all had access to the stock, and under the counter were boxes, tissue, gift tags and the famous gold-colored wrapping cord—all at the ready. New indirect lighting highlighted the space. The completed area used for retail purposes was approximately 2,700,000 square feet, or an approximate sixty-three acres. Field's had its own laundry service in the store, where fresh linens were prepared daily to supply all the restaurants with freshly ironed tablecloths, napkins, aprons, cook's jackets, towels and other necessities. At one time, Field's had an automatic telephone switchboard with twenty full-time operators to handle hundreds of calls a day, making it the largest private switchboard in the world.

Field's had a spacious waiting room with comfortable easy chairs. There were writing desks, as well as a completely complimentary supply of stationery and envelopes. There was a special clock made by German clock maker August Hahl that showed the times in Chicago, New York, Havana, London, Paris, Berlin, Manila, Tokyo, Honolulu and San Francisco.

The kitchens prepared all the delicious food for all the restaurants in the store. The bakery made all the cakes, cookies, rolls, coffee cakes, etc., for the restaurants and also sold them in the store's bakery. And the big copper kettle with melted chocolate was for the skilled candy handlers to hand dip each piece of famous Frango mints. These activities were all done on the thirteenth floor. In 1999, the candy kitchen was moved to a larger off-site facility. It still uses the same recipe, and the mints are now sold at Macy's.

In 1929, the Marshall Field's store purchased the Seattle-based Frederick and Nelson Company department store, along with its secret recipe. The Frango dessert at that time was a frozen ice cream treat until a candy maker created a mint candy truffle. This was brought to State Street, and the rest is history. More than one million pounds of Frango mints are sold yearly. Throughout the years, different flavors were made, and many are still available today at Macy's. There was dark chocolate mint, double chocolate mint, caramel, toffee, raspberry, rum, coffee, lemon, almond, coconut, orange and sugar free. Which is your favorite? Subsequently, with Frango's popularity, Field's promoted more products: dessert toppings, cookies, cocoa, teas, coffee, liqueurs and the Frango ice cream pie. Chicago is one of the candy capitals in the world. Some of the candy makers with a Chicago background were Tootsie Roll, O'Henry's, Wrigley Gum, Blommers Chocolate, World's Finest, Jelly Belly and the Ferrera Pan Candy Company.

The kitchens were equipped with all the apparatus necessary to supply the store's many restaurants, with efficient chefs and workers doing the prep work to give each customer a meal to remember. Among the food items prepared daily were 500 chickens, 250 pounds of butter, 180 dozen eggs and 150 pounds of coffee. It was said that "the law of averages works out so perfectly that the food managers could have estimated with amazing accuracy just how many chicken pot pies (one of Field's famous original dishes) will be called for on a given day, be it Monday or Thursday in rain or sunshine." These, as with many other well-known specialties, were seldom short and had few leftovers.

Up on the thirteenth floor was a little city in itself, bustling with all its support systems connecting to the various services and departments throughout the store. This floor housed the workrooms and studios. The carpenters' shop built all the "special needs" as they came up, including doing any store repairs and preparing scale models for the famous Christmas windows. Ice machines had the capacity to make two hundred tons of ice daily and supplied refrigeration for the fur storage vaults, drinking fountains, tearooms, restaurants and kitchens. Years later, it filtered air conditioning throughout the store.

MARKETPLACE

The Pantry started in the 1950s. It was based on an epicurean marketplace that someone might come across in Europe. It stocked hard-to-find gourmet foods and ingredients. It was a gourmet shopper's paradise, offering different salad dressings or the famous in-house Thousand Island dressing served in the Walnut Room, Strasbourg pâté de foie gras, eighteen varieties of honey, teas, coffee, spices, biscuits, pasta, pastries, canned and dry soups, cookies and much more. Wine and spirits were sold in later years, and the name was changed to a more popular-sounding one: Field's Marketplace. The Marketplace was on the seventh floor, as well as in the basement, or lower level. It accommodated the quick-food shopper with prepared foods, meals, sandwiches and an assortment of snacks, salads, soups and beverages to go.

THE 28TH SHOP

The 28th Shop had its formal opening on the elegant evening of September 30, 1941. Five hundred of the Midwest elite received engraved invitations from Mr. and Mrs. Hughston McBain. Field's welcoming committee was dressed in green and gold uniforms. To honor their guests, a butler announced them as they entered through the grand foyer and passed into the party. Champagne was served. Searchlights were outside, spreading the sky with white shafts of light, indicating that something extra exciting was happening inside the building. Howard Vincent O'Brien, a *Chicago Daily News* columnist, wrote, "It was like a Hollywood Premiere, a stream of high hats poured from a succession of limousines, while the flash bulbs winded merrily."

In the first year of the 28th Shop, sales reached $500,000. A woman could purchase a simple housecoat or an evening gown. The success of the shop was its service to women. It had mirror-lined walls with oak paneling and trim. It is interesting to note that the same man, Joseph Platt, who designed this 28th Shop also designed the sets for the movie *Gone With the Wind*. He was hired by Field's to design a space that would "Wow!" its customers—a place where famous dress designers like Hatie Carnegie, Nettie Rosenstein, Adrian and the likes would be proud to show off their designs.

Platt came up with a large room with twenty-eight individual smaller rooms circling the central salon. The entrance was through a beige oval foyer. To reach the 28th Shop on the sixth floor, you had to go to the Washington side of the building, whereupon a special elevator would whisk you upstairs. The doors of the private elevator would open to the foyer of the shop.

At the State Street level, there was an extraordinary gentleman/doorman named Charles Pritzlaff, who knew the customers who drove up in their fancy cars by name. "Charlie's Door" was one

Charles Pritzlaff, age eighty-one, celebrated his fifty-fifth anniversary as a doorman for Marshall Field's in 1952. "Charlie," as his guests would call him, handled the exclusive 28th Shop at the Washington Street entrance. He was known by many famous people, including the Queen of Romania. He became so popular that Emily Kimbrough mentioned him in her book about Marshall Field's, entitled *Through Charlie's Door*. *Courtesy of Macy's, Inc./Arthur C. Allen, Stadler Studios.*

of the unique little extras Marshall Field's was noted for. He would know all the ladies' comings and goings. He took care of every detail they needed and would be discreet in doing so. He was so kind and professional that it was said that during the holidays they would remember him with small tokens of their gratitude. These ladies considered the 28th Shop a home away from home, where they could have lunch and get their hair and makeup done—all at Field's.

The 28th Shop featured top fashions from New York and Europe. This included exclusive high-fashion designs. Christian Dior and a very young Yves Saint Laurent both made their first trips to America, and to Chicago, to visit the 28th Shop in the fall of 1957. The name "28th Shop" comes from the street number: 28 East Washington Street.

The Narcissus Room

Closed in 1987, the Narcissus Room was on the seventh floor on the northeast Wabash side of the building. It had a wonderful, clear view of Lake Michigan over which to enjoy a delicious lunch. In the center of the room was a delightful marble fountain surrounded by marble floor ties with refreshing cool water and topped by a bronze statue of Narcissus designed by Chicagoan Leonard Crunelle (1872–1950).

According to the *American Heritage Dictionary*, "Narcissus was a youth from Greek mythology who pined away in love for his own image in a pool of water and was transformed into the flower that bears his name."

Leonard Crunelle studied the arts in Paris and was a protégé of sculptor Loredo Taft, who had a workshop at the University of Chicago. Leonard Crunelle was a member of the oldest social club, the Cliff Dwellers, and exhibited one of his many works at the Art Institute of Chicago from 1897 to 1918. Another of his outstanding works, along with the Narcissus statue, was the Lincoln Tomb in Springfield. The Narcissus Room was converted into an employee lunchroom and later a special events center.

THE CRYSTAL PALACE

The Crystal Palace Ice Cream Parlor was founded in 1975 on the third floor and was later moved to the seventh floor. It was like visiting an old ice cream parlor of the past or a section of an old dime store that had stools with a soda fountain. The waitresses wore white uniforms with white- and pink-striped aprons. Special dessert dishes, glasses and spoons were used. Each treat came with a small home-baked cookie. Reading the menu was like a trip back to your favorite old malt shop from the old neighborhood. The hot fudge sundae was a staple, as was the banana split. The room itself had small, round metal tables with replicas of matching soda fountain chairs. Or you could sit at the fountain with its stained glass and mirrored decorative backdrop, enjoying a delicious chocolate malt. White and pink tiles covered the floors and walls. There were large mirrors and green plants hanging in baskets. It was a most pleasant place to go to.

In 1932, in connection with the city's celebration of the Century of Progress Exhibition (1933–34), Marshall Field's installed new electrical, stainless steel escalators manufactured by Westinghouse and Company. The sleek, skinny, art deco escalators were monitored during peak store times and during holidays with a staff of Andy Frain uniformed ushers/guards. "Please hold the hand rail!" was heard constantly. The ushers were helping customers on and off the escalators. In 1936, the Wabash Avenue building had escalators installed.

The Marshall Field's transportation delivery services grew with the times, as well. At the beginning, there were all the usual horse-and-buggy delivery wagons. Depending on the size of the merchandise, larger carts and carriages would be used. Then the horse-drawn torch delivery wagons were used, followed by the pre–World War I "sleek electrics" in the early 1900s. They were somewhat motorized, small electric trucks with narrow bodies that could make average-sized deliveries. Each driver was taught strict rules and regulations. They were the representatives of Marshall Field's every time they had contact with the public and were always to remember their motto: "Be on time. Be correct. Deliver neat parcels." Delivery service was a no-charge service that started back in 1872. By 1913, Field's had a fleet of 188 motorized trucks and still used its 142 horse-drawn delivery wagons, pulled by its 375 available horses. Delivery boundaries went as far as a thirty-five-mile radius from the State Street store. Moving

The Crystal Palace in 1975 was first located on the third floor and then relocated to the seventh floor, with a larger menu of ice cream treats. The stained-glass windows and gleaming white tile floors welcomed shoppers to indulge in cool ice cream rewards after hours of shopping. *Courtesy of Macy's, Inc.*

The Marshall Field's celebration promoting the World's Fair of 1933–34. Various flags of the participating countries were hung high over the main aisle. *Courtesy of Macy's, Inc.*

forward in the transportation delivery method, Field's purchased two London taxicab vehicles. They were painted with various shades of green stripes and made quite an appearance on the streets of Chicago in 2003—sadly, this is another page of the past that faded away.

Still another reminder of growth was the wood-paneled drugstore on the first floor, complete with its own pharmacist to fill prescriptions. And by 1937, air conditioning had been introduced and installed to enhance the shopping experience of Field's customers.

All of the "firsts" introduced by Marshall Field's were imaginative and diligently geared to the customer's wants and the public's needs. Improvements became indispensable as the years passed: the first European buying offices, the first personal shopper, the first store post office, the first bank of telephone operators, the first concept of "book signings," the first set of display window decorations, the first use of escalators, the first bridal registry, the first revolving credit cards, the first famous theme windows at Christmastime and the first use of store Christmas trees (still a tradition today). Field's success was thanks, in part, to the gifted specialists and skilled employees who diligently performed their jobs, each taking care of the smallest or most minute detail for each and every customer. A shopper could rest assured that his special order would be handled, wrapped, shipped, repaired or corrected promptly, all in a professional manner.

THE TREND HOUSE

The original Trend House began in 1936 and showed affordable home designs. The Trend House was a grouping of mainly four rooms with approximately three thousand square feet. Twice a year, the entire suite of rooms was completely designed and built with furniture, art and fixtures, each display unique in concept and extravagant in execution. Soon, it became a place where high-priced top designers showcased their wares to influence the customer concerning the trends of the day. Customers were encouraged to walk through the rooms at their leisure and take notes on the furniture, accessories, light fixtures and details. Any and all ideas could be ordered or purchased from Field's. The Trend House is no longer. In 1990, Forman Publishing published a fantastic, out-of-print coffee table book about the Trend House, entitled *Epoustouflant: The Style of David Snyder* and written by the late David Snyder, vice-president of home fashions/interior design. Mr. Snyder was one of many influential designers who took a turn at redecorating the Trend House over the years.

CANDY CANE LANE

Candy Cane Lane—that fabulous and engaging toy department on the fourth floor—was for children of any age. There were toys that were thought provoking, fun and entertaining. There were technical toys and kits for young boys, like erector sets and microscopes. Over the years, there was a magician and a puppeteer to put on small shows for the children. The store had sophisticated science kits and chess games, stuffed animals and toy soldiers, miniature orchestra instruments and unique, interesting toys from all parts of the world. The German- and American-made train sets laid out and displayed on massive tables throughout the department encouraged everyone to stop and enjoy running the trains full throttle around the displays.

And then there were the little girls' dreams and wishes. The doll collection was superior, from rag dolls to Madam Alexander—the full gambit—with metal or wooden dollhouses and miniature furniture to go with them. There were also sewing and baking kits, doll clothing, beds, tea sets and dishes; toy vacuums, brooms and entire miniature kitchens; bead and jewelry kits, games, coloring books—and the list goes on and on. You would ask for something for your birthday and hope Mom and Dad would go back to Field's to surprise you.

Field's had a natural knack for attending to children. It had a special playroom with an attending nurse to watch children while their parents shopped. Kids could have "playsuits" to wear that fit their imaginations, like cowboy outfits. The restaurants offered special children's menus and had special giveaways throughout years. Marshall Field published the *Juvenile World Magazine*. The store had a special barber for the little ones that made them unafraid to get a haircut. It had a Young People's Theater as well. The children were delighted to receive mail for themselves. A toy cardboard treasure chest was a small mail giveaway that had miniature paper treasures to cut out and place back inside the toy chest: a car, a doll, a miniature stove, trucks, a dollhouse, a bicycle, a train set, musical instruments, stuffed animals and more. Coincidentally, the mailer indicated that these toys could all be purchased on your next trip to Field's. The toy department was to the child a land of enchantment and to the grownup an escape from the everyday world. The year-round toy selection of Field's was known far and wide for its size and distinguished quality.

And, finally, the basement was filled with quality merchandise at moderate prices. The bargain basement, later to be called the "lower level," was filled with items for the average workingman or housewife. It had bargains—that is, "older stock,"

A cardboard treasure chest promotion mailed out to children to cut out and have a pretend toy chest with all their favorite toys inside. The banjo instrument was $7.50, as was the toy truck. Perhaps you would pick one of the automobile models? *Robert P. Ledermann, private collection.*

"after their time" or seasonal merchandise that the buyers had overbought and had to "move out" and take a loss on the price. It had "factory seconds"—products that were manufactured with high quality but for some reason had a slight flaw and could not be sold as "perfect." Field's basement had a jewelry department; a candy shop; shoe repair; fashion accessories; women, men and children's clothing; shoes; and coats. There was a juice bar and frozen ice cream area. There were fabric and notions, rug remnants, linens and bedding, housewares and baby's needs departments. In later years, a food court called the Marshall Field's Marketplace, a gourmet shop, was added. Pedestrians who had come in from the State Street subway, which was connected to the basement of Marshall Field's, had access to the Marketplace as well.

Marshall Field's fabulous flower show of 1960 filled the air inside with fragrance, and a blanket of multicolored flowers surrounded all the counters on the main aisle, as well as the State Street windows from Randolph to Washington. Year after year, these shows have attracted garden clubs and gardeners to see what selections of different flowers would be highlighted. Today, Macy's continues this wonderful springtime tradition. *Courtesy of Chicago Sun-Times Newspaper Media/Archival Department.*

As a side note, even State Street itself was closed off to through traffic from 1940 to 1941 for construction of the State Street subway. On October 16, 1943, the first train ran beneath State Street. This transformed Chicago's transportation problem. It was definitely an amazing change to State Street.

The bargain basement of today doesn't have many bargains. The lower level has an array of housewares, small repair shops, food courts, washrooms and a bakery, as well as a better-quality watch repair service and eyeglasses shop. The bakery that was on the seventh floor is now on the lower level. Pots, pans, luggage and a small section of the book department were moved down to the lower level as well. Today, the book department is leased from Macy's by Barbara's Books.

These conversions to update and modernize the lower level were completed in the late 1980s. Throughout the years, some of the specialty departments have come and gone, including the music and record shop, with its console televisions and radios; the coin and stamp shop, with its knowledgeable clerks; the garden and outdoor furniture department; and even the fireplace and accessory departments.

CELEBRITY QUOTES ABOUT MARSHALL FIELD'S

It is impossible to end this chapter on Marshall Field's State Street store without including some words from famous people summing up their experiences and gratitude:

At last—a dream come true—All night long in my favorite department store: Marshall Field's! With "unconditional love."
—Kathy Bates, April 20, 2000

To our friends at Marshall Field's. Thank you for your friendship and community initiative.
—Kenneth Cole, December 2001:

Thank you. Love Liza.
—Liza Minnelli, May 12, 1988

To my friends at Marshall Field's. Love and blessings.
—Ginger Rodgers, October 16, 1991

Thanks for a lovely day.
—Audrey Meadows, October 11, 1994

What a great store!
—Payne Stewart, circa 1997

To my friends at Marshall Field's, Thank You! Great Cooking!
—Emeril Lagasse, October 17, 1997

Bon Appetite!
—Julia Child, October 11, 1999

Always!
—Red Skelton, 1968

In all my travels, I have found no better favorite for good food than here at Field's. The Mount Vernon of the West, a haven for food and rest. Marshall Field's food is only exceeded by its genuine hospitality.
—Duncan Hines

Gratefully to Marshall Field's, the greatest store in the world, where personalized service makes it possible to get what you want anywhere, any time.
—Sally Rand, 1941

One of my favorite places, Marshall Field's.
—Harold Lloyd, 1938:

The delightful hospitality of this wonderful Marshall Field's soon eases everything.
—Edward Everett Horton, 1939

To Marshall Field, one institution to another.
—Eddie Cantor, 1943:

I couldn't come to Chicago without visiting Marshall Field's.
—Louella O. Parsons, 1944

For Marshall Field's—Our admiration always.
—Lucille Ball and Desi Arnaz, 1950

On January 10, 1952, Marshall Field's celebrated one hundred years of fashion. Honoring the centennial was chairman of the board Houston McBain and a special cake surrounded by fashion models wearing various styles of clothing throughout the years. *Courtesy of* Chicago Sun-Times *Newspaper Media/Archival Department.*

Marshall Field's is my favorite store.
—Duncan Hines, 1950

Best Wishes.
—Orson Wells, 1957

I have been to Paris, London, Rome, Vienna, Budapest, New York, Los Angeles, etc.,
and this is still my favorite place to shop.
—Louella O. Parsons

This is the greatest store on earth.
—Milo Vagge (bag puncher with Ringling Brothers and Barnum & Bailey
Circus), 1937

To the great house in which as a boy and man I spent twenty-five years of my life.
I always give my happiest congratulations and wishes for continual greatest success.
—Harry Gordon Selfridge, April 25, 1932

To the greatest institution in Chicago and the kindest.
—Mrs. Charles W. Wrigley

Department store—or exhibition of beautiful things—it is hard to decide!
— Lotte Zilesch, Berlin, June 1935

The finest store in all the world is where I shop when I come to Chicago.
— Al Jolson

To travel is to possess the world, but we always come back to Chicago—which is a
suburb of Marshall Field's.
—Burton Holmes, March 2, 1938:

My first visit to Marshall Field's has been a thrill for me.
— Paulette Goddard, May 17, 1943

Where does the West begin? Marshall Field's!
— Sister Donatilla, New York:

This is a beautiful store. Love Shirley Temple.
—Shirley Temple (aged nine years), 1938

Me Too!
—Jack Benny, September 25, 1939

From Florence, Italy, to Marshall Field's.
—Enrico Caruso Jr., October 28, 1941

To this epitome of civilization—Marshall Field's.
—Frank Lloyd Wright, May 12, 1942:

My sincere best wishes to a wonderful store.
—Kim Novak, 1960

My first visit to the greatest store in the world.
— Jack Dempsey, February 18, 1932

One brick at a time…

4

MARSHALL FIELD'S AND CHRISTMAS

Christmas in Chicago was Marshall Field's, and Marshall Field's was Christmas in Chicago. Field's had many slogans throughout the years, including "The store with the Christmas spirit" and "Christmas isn't Christmas without a day at Field's."

In 1907, the bus boys brought a small fresh fir tree into the Tea Room/Walnut Room and trimmed it themselves with ornaments they brought from home. The customers enjoyed it and looked forward to seeing it each year. This fresh tree from the employees lasted fifteen years, until Field's created the "tree department" concept. The tree tradition grew into a blossoming fir that was forty-five feet high, with a wonderful group of employees making marvelous ornaments for it. These employees sat at massive long tables, hand making each ornament.

Late in autumn, team members would head out to either Lake Superior County in Minnesota or the Upper Peninsula of Michigan to select the tree with the aid of a professional timber expert. A symmetrical blossoming fir tree, seventy feet tall, would be selected. Carefully, the top forty-five feet were looped and lowered by block and tackle to prevent any damage to the branches, which were bound tightly to the tree trunk. A bulldozer truck broke a path through the forest, and the tree was hauled by sled to a nearby railroad flatcar to take it to Chicago. While the last customers left the store, usually on a Saturday, the tree handlers would jump to action to receive the tree at the store. Chicago streets were blocked off to permit a huge tractor-trailer to carry the tree to the Randolph and State Street entrance doors, which were removed to enable the thick base of the tree to be pulled through into the first floor. The base of the tree was safely packed in peat moss and slid neatly through the aisle. It was then hoisted and guided up to the seventh floor, through the "North Light Well" and into the Walnut Room. The former fishpond fountain

Workmen brought a fresh fir tree through the Randolph Street entrance, circa 1960s. The doors were removed to allow the tree to be carried into the store. *Courtesy of* Chicago Sun-Times *Newspaper Media/Archival Department.*

in the center of the room was drained. Block and tackle was used to set the tree in the center of the fountain, secured from the ceiling, where it could be enjoyed by shoppers throughout the holiday season.

When the fresh evergreen tree was introduced, it created some problems. One year, all the needles fell off, and it had to be replaced quickly. Still another year, real candy was used as part of the trimming, and in the morning, the tree was absolutely shimmering with mice. It was apparently quite a sight! A fireman was required to guard the tree and keep a watchful eye for any fire that might threaten it. He would quietly sit to the side, equipped with the means to extinguish any fire. To help alleviate the threat of fire, an elaborate sprinkler system was put in place. Three water pipes were run through the tree, and eight fire hoses were at the ready nearby. It was said that "you would never have to worry if the tree caught on fire, but you might drown from all the water." Just think of the destruction, let alone the panic and confusion, a disaster like this could have caused!

Due to the constant danger, it was decided to switch to an artificial tree to ease the minds of all concerned. In 1963, Field's commissioned Charles Cohen of the Colonial Decorative Display Co., Inc., of New York to design such a tree. His partner, Irving "Gus" Mittelmark, was delighted upon its completion to Field's exact specifications. Field's was glad it had selected the company and invited Colonial back each year to instruct and oversee the tree setup, with the help of a group of Field's employees.

The tree handlers erected the Great Tree and secured it. Still others assembled all the limbs and branches. The electricians wired and placed the lights. Finally, the tree trimmers hung all the ornaments. These design department employees made approximately five thousand ornaments each year. They would decorate the tree, starting with the top portion, using the smaller ornaments; then moving down to the middle section, with the medium-sized ornaments; and finally placing the larger ornaments at the base and bottom. The larger branches were as long as fifteen feet and weighed as much as fifty pounds each. The tree was constructed with three fifteen-

In 1961, the fir tree was taken to the "North Light Well," where it was hoisted up through the well and onto the seventh floor. *Courtesy of* Chicago Sun-Times *Newspaper Media/Archival Department.*

Upon arrival in 1962, the tree was placed at the center of the Walnut Room in the old fishpond fountain. *Courtesy of* Chicago Sun-Times *Newspaper Media/ Archival Department.*

foot sections of pipe with receiving poles (branches) that stuck into each section. An average-sized man standing on one of these shanks (branches) would easily be supported. Four stories of scaffolding would surround the tree, and the decorators would work their magic.

The dimensions of the tree were told to me by Mr. Cohen himself in 1980, on one of his return visits to help with the tree's setup. The tree was forty-five feet high from the fountain base up to the ceiling. Cohen was a fine, hardworking man who took personal pride in his work—so much so that he guaranteed Field's that the tree would last thirty years. Even after thirty-nine years, it was still as sturdy as ever. Customers (not knowing it wasn't real) would gaze up at it and wonder aloud how could it stay so fresh day after day. They were convinced they could smell the fresh scent of pine.

Marshall Field's fresh fir Christmas tree in 1962 was untied, secured and ready to be decorated. *Courtesy of* Chicago Sun-Times *Newspaper Media/ Archival Department.*

When Target Corp. took control of the Field's store from Batus, Inc. (1982–1990), it decided that a new artificial tree was needed. The Target Corp. maintained Field's integrity from 1990 to 2004. In 2003, Target's new Christmas tree made its official debut, along with, for the first time, corporate sponsorship: the tree was covered in Waterford crystal ornaments. In years past, the tree would have a new theme each year; this theme was also sometimes reflected in the window display. One year it could be all Santa; another year it could be a Victorian theme with dainty lace ornaments, a toy tree, a circus tree, a clown tree with Bozo or an Uncle Mistletoe tree. In recent years, ornaments have been geared with a promotional theme, through which the store reflects a particular product or character, such as Harry Potter, Paddington Bear, the Grinch, Swarovski crystal, Wedgwood, Vera

Above, left: In 1980, the Colonial Decorative Display Co. came back to Chicago to help employees of Marshall Field's place branches on the first artificial tree and helped with the completion of the tree in the Walnut Room. *Photo © Robert P. Ledermann.*

Above, right: *From left to right*: my wife, Mrs. Annette Ledermann; Mrs. Charles Cohen; and Mr. Charles Cohen, the creator of the first artificial tree. This photo was taken as the tree was being prepared in the Walnut Room after store hours. *Photo © Robert P. Ledermann.*

Wang and even Martha Stewart. Sadly, there was no need to continue with the employee tradition of hand-made ornaments.

In past years, the popularity and success of Field's was tied to its beautiful Christmas windows. The public couldn't wait to see what the store was going to do in these display windows. Of utmost importance was creating the theme windows each year with a freshness of ideas to outdo the last set of windows. Generally, the theme was created early in January. Colors and materials were thought of, and a scale model of each window was presented for the executives' final approval. The window display team then took on the task of replicating these models into full-sized proportions

In 1980, scaffolding surrounded the tree and the artisans from the Interior Display Department as they placed hand-made ornaments on the branches. *Photo © Robert P. Ledermann.*

to fit into each window. From Labor Day on, the window display department worked full time, completing each of the thirteen windows until they were all unveiled to the public, usually a few weeks before Thanksgiving. Only the finest materials and meticulous workmanship went into the planning of these windows.

In 2004–05, the May Department Store Group purchased Field's from Target and ran it for a short while, until Federated Department Stores (Macy's) bought it.

In 2009, Macy's wanted to create its own tree for the Walnut Room and at the same time eliminate the time-consuming hours it took to erect it. A Macy's executive told me that two new trees were manufactured to Macy's specifications, one for the Walnut Room in Chicago and the other for the Macy's store in Harold Square in New York. The efficiency of the new tree ran circles around the preparation time of the older trees. It would take days and nights with various crews to do the work on the old trees. It takes Macy's staff thirty-six hours to install the new tree and only twelve hours to remove it completely at the end of the holiday season, usually in mid-January. As of 2011, there have been some 103 different trees set up and decorated for the public's enjoyment. This new Macy's tree is thirty-eight feet high with a seven-foot topper and weighs 1,450 pounds. It is unique in that it actually assembles from the top down. The star at the tip is installed first and then the top section is moved into place and joined by another section—and so on until it is completed. There are a total of eight sections. It never rests on the base of the fountain but actually hangs from the ceiling. There are sixty-six hundred LED lights illuminating the tree, with thirty-four hundred illuminating the topper alone. The words you see projected onto the base are from theatrical lighting on the eighth floor. These lights are called "Gobo" projections. A total of twenty-one different ornaments cover the tree. The Walnut Room, where the tree is displayed, was

The interior display artisans sat at long tables on the thirteenth floor, crafting hand-made ornaments for the tree. *Photo © Robert P. Ledermann.*

originally called the Tea Room and then the Walnut Grill. Located at the southwest corner of the State Street store, it is a delightful place for a delicious meal.

The Circassian-Russian walnut paneling and crystal chandeliers with matching crystal wall sconces enhance the beauty of the Walnut Room. The room has a warm but elegant charm, with plush carpeting, linen tablecloths and napkins matched with silver-plated utensils. Fresh flowers usually welcome diners to relax at the square tables and comfortable chairs. Huge plate glass windows enable customers to look out at State Street. Sometimes a group of musicians plays classical selections. During the holidays, carolers walk about and sing Christmas carols, or you might catch a glimpse of the "Little People" with their bobbling oversized heads and small bodies or the Jingle Elf in full costume passing out rewards for good deeds. The

The Great Tree in the Walnut Room in 2003, installed by Target Corp. This was only the second artificial tree to be used since the early 1960s. It had crystal ornaments created and designed by Waterford. *Courtesy of Macy's, Inc.*

wait staff is pleasant and knowledgeable of the menu selections.

Margaret Cimoli was one of the wonderful ladies who started working for Field's in 1952. She just wanted a part-time job and replied to a newspaper ad for help in the Veranda Room, where she served lunches for ninety-nine cents. She remembers when the part-time days became full-time and all the special parties when she wore a female tuxedo. Families would come and request to be seated in her section. This sweet lady stayed on for fifty-five years. Marshall Field's appreciated her loyalty with various gifts commemorating her "years of service."

At Christmastime, placing the Great Tree in the middle of the fountain in the Walnut Room made Marshall Field's the holiday centerpiece of Chicago, with all the bells and whistles. Throughout the years, the fountain structure has boasted different promotions or seasonal themes. I can remember once there was a twenty-seven-foot-high HMS *Pussy Willow*, a moving mechanical contraption with collections of bits and bobs, wire, wheels—everything but the kitchen sink—in continuous motion. At Easter, a huge basket filled with flowers was on display—but then, there always were beautiful flowers or lovely green ferns surrounding the fountain.

The menus changed from year to year. Children had a novelty menu all to themselves to select from. Most of the food choices printed on the menus at Christmas had holiday names, even the desserts and cocktails. Throughout the years, the "star" of the menu was Sarah Haring's chicken potpie. She was a clerk in the millinery department. She had a strong group of ladies who continued to purchase their hats from her alone. They trusted her, and they appreciated her judgment of whether the hats were complimentary on them. One day, she overheard some ladies ponder the idea that there should be a place to sit and have a small meal. Sarah offered to share

Above: The topper of Macy's 2009 new Christmas tree. *Courtesy of Macy's, Inc.*

Opposite: Macy's 2009 new artificial tree, with its beautiful silver and shades of blue ornaments, sparkled and delighted the guests in the Walnut Room restaurant. The wonderful Christmas tree tradition continues for the next generation of Chicagoans to enjoy. The reflecting words of "Imagine," "Wish," "Believe" and "Dream" surrounded the base. *Courtesy of Macy's, Inc.*

Left: Margaret Cimoli only wanted a part-time job in 1952 but stayed more than fifty-five years, serving customers with her beautiful smile and warm personality. *Photo courtesy of Margaret Cimoli.*

Below: Margaret Cimoli serving in the Walnut Room. *Photo courtesy of Margaret Cimoli.*

the lunch she had brought from home: her chicken potpie. She set up a small table off to the side, and the ladies enjoyed the meal. Word spread. The very next day, more of her customers were at her counter looking for lunch.

In came manager Harry Selfridge, who quickly recognized that this was a win-win situation. He enthusiastically supported Haring's idea to serve her chicken potpie for lunch and went straight up to promote the idea to Mr. Field and the "boys." They made the comment, "Give the lady what she wants." Sarah Haring's impromptu lunch service developed into a fine restaurant, the beginnings of the famous Walnut Room. What could be simpler: a comfortable place for hungry shoppers to relax and enjoy a delicious meal. Waitresses wore white aprons over black long-sleeved dress uniforms with stiff white cuffs and collars. Their hair was neatly managed and trimmed, and a white cap and black sensible work shoes were a must. "High tea" was served after lunch hours finished. It had fewer customers but usually catered to female shoppers. The menu consisted of small finger sandwiches, nut breads, jams and jellies, scones, cookies, small tarts and

One of the novelty children's menus, circa 1950s, was called "Eddie the Elephant." It had a selection of four choices: A fifty-five-cent lunch had chicken or lamb, vegetables, ice cream or fruit compote, a cookie and milk or cocoa. For forty-five cents, one could have chicken croquettes, and for thirty-five cents, a fresh cold vegetable plate with bread and bacon. A peanut butter and raspberry jam sandwich was fifteen cents. *Robert P. Ledermann, private collection.*

pastries and perhaps a selection of fresh seasonal fruits with cream and the best collection of imported teas. The potpie was forty cents—or with all white meat, forty-five cents—and a breaded lamb chop with mint jelly was forty cents.

Gordon Selfridge hired Arthur Valair Fraser, whose background was in dry goods in the small town of Creston, Iowa. Fraser was born in Quebec, Canada. His reputation for good work in window displays preceded him, and Selfridge wasted no time in getting him into Field's. With his natural flair for design, the Field's windows came to life. Fraser was known as "the dean of display" and became famous for his opulent windows. He had a group of display artists, painters and carpenters—even a plaster molder—who listened to his meticulous instructions to prepare the perfect displays. These display windows totaled more than sixty around the building complex. They were educational as well as decorative. They changed from season to season and presented a panorama of color in artistry, fabric and fashion. They won awards for beauty and uniqueness of design. After decades of loyal contributions to Field's, Fraser's reign ended in 1944, and John Moss stepped into service as his successor, continuing the legacy of the Marshall Field's windows.

In 1944, John Moss became director of design. The first set of thirteen Christmas-themed windows was Clement Moore's "A Visit from St. Nicholas" ("The Night Before Christmas"). They were such a popular success that they were repeated in 1945. These windows were so welcomed by the public that John Moss decided to make something completely different that would belong to Field's alone. He contacted his assistant, Johanna Osborne, about his idea. She went to her summer home in Williams Bay, Wisconsin, to relax and think about the project. She thought about her elderly uncle Ola, from Oslo, Norway, and his round, happy face. She thought of her fondness for Charles Dickens and his characters, and she thought of *Arabian Nights* (by Sir Richard Burton). She combined these ideas and told her husband, Addis (who was a teacher at the Art Institute of Chicago), her thoughts of creating "Uncle Mistletoe." He would have white hair and a happy face with black bushy eyebrows. He would wear a black top hat, a bright red cape and black trousers. He would be somewhat like a Pickwickian character from a Dickens novel combined with her favorite uncle Ola. Addis came up with the perfect sketches. Uncle Mistletoe wore a white aviator scarf and had a pair of white gauzy wings that helped him fly about when he was on an adventure with his magic carpet or just keeping an eye on the children to see if they were being good and then reporting back to Santa as his ambassador.

Monday morning came. Johanna took Addis's sketches to Mr. Moss and his boss, Lawrence Sizer, vice-president of finance and director of public relations. They originally thought the character's name should be Uncle Marshall, but it was finally decided to keep the name Uncle Mistletoe. During this meeting, it was also decided that a story poem suitable for the Christmas windows should be developed. They called in Helen McKenna, a copywriter for Field's. Together, Johanna and Helen created the very first set of Christmas-themed story-poem windows entitled "A Christmas Dream" in 1946. The story was about a brother and sister named Jim-Jam and Joann who were patterned after Johanna's nephew and niece. These youngsters dreamed that Uncle Mistletoe appeared at their window on his magic carpet and took them up to the North Pole for a visit with Santa and his reindeer. They visited Santa and were rewarded with Kindness Club buttons, which they pinned on their

This was the first public appearance of Uncle Mistletoe in a Marshall Field's Christmas window, in 1946–47, entitled "A Christmas Dream." Note the striped framing of the window. The following text appears under the window: "They hadn't slept long when an odd little guy a' riding a carpet flew in and said hi! My name's Uncle Mistletoe! Just take my hand, we're going on a journey to Santa Claus Land." *Courtesy of Macy's, Inc.*

coats. They awoke in the last set of double windows at the corner of Washington and State Streets and told their parents of their adventure with Uncle Mistletoe. But was it really a dream? Their buttons were still on their coats. Special treatment and care was given to every detail to ensure that these windows were a triumph. They were repeated again in 1947.

Just as Dickens's character Mr. Fezziwig surely needed a Mrs. Fezziwig, Uncle Mistletoe needed a partner, a wife and a friend. Aunt Holly was all of these and more. She was the sweet and affectionate character who stood at his side in 1948 in the Christmas windows "A Christmas Surprise." Aunt Holly had white hair piled neatly in a bun on top of her head. She wore reading glasses, a red dress with a cameo pin at her neckline, a white apron and a matching red cape. Her favorite hobbies were making cookies for Uncle Mistletoe and the reindeer and sewing

Left: Johanna Osborne, October 1980, with the original sketches of Uncle Mistletoe by her husband, Addis. *Photo © Robert P. Ledermann.*

Below: Johanna and Addis Osborne, creators of the Christmas characters Uncle Mistletoe and Aunt Holly, in their summer home in Williams Bay, Wisconsin, with an original prototype figure in October 1980. *Photo © Robert P. Ledermann.*

clothes for Uncle Mistletoe.

As of 1948, the Mistletoes were recognized as permanent residents of "Cozy Cloud Cottage," the place where little girls and boys stood in line at Christmastime to visit with Santa Claus. Uncle Mistletoe became one of Marshall Field's greatest promotional advertisements for the store. He was used not only at the Christmas holiday but also sometimes during the Easter season. His popularity grew, and he had his own television program from Chicago, originating from WENR (now WLS Channel 7), penthouse studios in the Chicago Civic Opera House. It aired Monday through Friday from 5:45 p.m. to 6:00 p.m. in the fall of 1948. It was called *The Adventures of Uncle Mistletoe*—a puppet show with the voice of the late Uncle Johnny Coons (the television and radio personality) as Uncle Mistletoe. The late Jennifer Holt played Aunt Holly. Together they would discuss the day's adventure. Jennifer's dad was the late Jack Holt, and her brother was the late Tim Holt. Both were cowboy actors in Hollywood pictures.

On the show, children met new puppet friends, including Otto the Elephant, Humphrey the Mouse, Michael O'Hara the Rabbit and Obadiah Pig. Doris Larson signed on after Jennifer left in 1951. She was called the "Look Out Lady." At the beginning of each program, she would pretend to be looking through a magic looking glass and would talk with Uncle Mistletoe about the past and the upcoming events of the day. Then, in 1952, the show moved over to WGN-TV Channel 9 on Tuesdays and Thursdays at 5:15 p.m.

To the right is a set of Uncle Mistletoe and Aunt Holly figures used in the Field's windows from 1970s on. These were made of hard rubber with hand-made felt clothing. Previously, hand-made Mistletoes were constructed of paper mache. The buttons were the three different Mistletoe buttons. The Kindness Club button on the left was mailed to children, the middle button was handed out by Santa and the right button was the special 1980s version used in the "Christmas Surprise" windows and is quite rare (note the "K" in "Klub" on this button). *Photo © Robert P. Ledermann.*

More puppet friends were added—among them Polly Dolly, Molio, Olio, Private Pepper and Aunt Holly—but the show only lasted a brief thirteen weeks.

Through his popularity, Marshall Fields sponsored a children's club called the Kindness Club. Children were encouraged to write to the club about their good deeds, and in return, they would receive a Kindness Club button, a copy of the song and a little note from Uncle Mistletoe. Field's used Uncle Mistletoe in seasonal newspaper ads that began traditionally on Thanksgiving Day. These ads would promote Uncle Mistletoe and at the same time advise and inform readers of the new supply of colorful Christmas gift boxes, gift certificates, trim-a-tree items, cards, wrapping paper and ornaments ready for purchase.

In the fall on 1982, I wrote an article for the Chicago Historical Society (today's Chicago History Museum) magazine, *Chicago History*, entitled "Uncle Mistletoe: A Chicago Christmas Tradition." I received a surprise phone call from Margo Moss, the daughter of John Moss, who succeeded Arthur Fraser as vice-president and design director at Marshall Field's. She was a graduate of Sarah Lawrence College and the Latin School and a member of the Women's Board of Rush-Presbyterian St. Luke's Medical Center, the Junior League of Chicago and the Junior Governing Board of the Chicago Symphony Orchestra. She was so delighted to read my kind words about her dad that she wanted to meet with me for lunch at the Casino Club.

In remembrance of both Margo and her father, I'm including the song she received upon becoming a member of the Kindness Club:

The Kindness Club Song

Uncle Mistletoe, says he, wants the boys and girls to be
In his Kindness Club to stay, if they're kind and good each day
Not just one day, not just two, but be kind the whole year through
Oh…
Do a kind deed, say a kind thing, smile a big smile, everyone sing,
Feel the wind of kindness blowing,
Watch the way the vane is going,
Uncle Mistletoe is glad,
When you help your Mom and Dad,
Polish your button, give it a rub,
Everyone's proud of the Kindness Club"

We remembered the three different kinds of Uncle Mistletoe buttons. There was the common button, which was given away when children visited with Santa. It was simple, displaying Uncle Mistletoe's face in color, and around the edge were the words "Uncle Mistletoe, Marshall Field & Company." These buttons were given away by the thousands and were probably tossed out. But if you were to find one today, you would still be lucky.

The second button was sent along with a letter on Field's stationery to any child who belonged to the Kindness Club. This button also had Uncle Mistletoe's face in color in the middle, with his name underneath. On top, around the edge, were the words "Kindness Club Inc.," and written at the lower edge was "Marshall Field & Company." The letter to the children read:

> *I read your letter telling me of your good deed. I want you to be a member of the Kindness Club Inc. and to wear this button.*
> *Now remember, kindness is more than just one good deed. Let this button help to remind you to do good deeds every day, and to keep on watching my adventures on your television set.*

The third button issued was a limited edition of one hundred exclusively used in the Christmas story windows in 1980. These buttons had the same Uncle Mistletoe face, only it was all in the color red. Over his head, on the top edge of the button, were the words "Uncle Mistletoes," and the bottom edge read "Kindness Klub." "Klub" is written with a "K" instead of a "C" to promote the special button.

Field's also mailed out to the kids a small, square paper pamphlet describing the complete set of windows of "A Christmas Dream" of 1946–47 and a round paper pamphlet describing the story from "A Party for Santa" from the 1951 windows. These were sent out to anyone who requested them.

During my luncheon with Margo Moss, our conversation turned to all the other memories she had—similar to my own—of going downtown as a child with her mom and dad and stopping in Field's to see Santa in Cozy Cloud Cottage. It seemed like the line waiting to see Santa was huge, but as children, it didn't feel too bad. Margo and her parents would have lunch in the Walnut Room and then go outside to look at all the other department store display windows along with the crowds.

That triggered a multitude of memories of all the different merchandise over the years, the Great Tree items, Uncle Mistletoe, the Walnut Room, the Santa Bears, all the traditional foods that were stocked and filled the shelves for the holiday shoppers and the store itself. There were numerous items sold concerning Uncle Mistletoe and Aunt Holly. Some of my favorite recollections, besides the hand puppets, were all the ornaments made throughout the years. The originals were from Germany, hand-blown and painted. They were the largest. A few years later, they were copied and made smaller, this time in Austria. After that, several

One of the Christmas windows of 1959 depicting a story in the massive Marshall Field's display windows on State Street. Uncle Mistletoe was made of paper mache. *Courtesy of* Chicago Sun-Times *Newspaper Media/Archival Department.*

different versions were made in Japan using different materials such as felt, glass, paper and cloth. The last group of Mistletoe ornaments was manufactured through Macy's and designed by Christopher Radko. There was a *Little Golden Book* and a very tall, thin, narrow book, a good copy of which is extremely hard to find today. It is entitled *A Tall Tale from the Adventures of Uncle Mistletoe, Humphrey Mouse and the Sky Scraper*, a story by Ray Chan, illustrated by William Newton in 1950.

There were lots of cookie jars, coloring books, snow globes, tree skirts, party goods, decanters and glassware, luncheon plates, mugs, cards, tea napkins, etc. Radko also made the Field's clock ornaments. Judith Jack produced marvelous bracelets, charms, pins and earrings featuring the clocks, trees and things in the Field's store. Mark McMahon painted watercolors and limited editions of images of the Great Tree, the Walnut Room and the store. Artist Rainy Bennett, who did various art projects, drew the newspaper ads and sketches of Uncle Mistletoe and Aunt Holly on Bing & Grondahl china—collector's plates. The Sebastian Miniature Co. created limited editions of figurines. The Chicago-based artist Jack Shimmerling made wonderful sketches, paintings and drawings—as well as other merchandise such as greeting cards and stationery—of the outside of Marshall Field's State Street store, Carson, Pirie, Scott & Company and the homes and mansions along Prairie Avenue.

Following the popularity of Uncle Mistletoe in 1973, Freddy Fieldmouse made his first appearance in the Christmas windows. The next year, his partner, Marsha, joined him, followed by the birth and christening of their four little ones: Flora, Fanny, Franklin and Forester. This window was entitled "The Greatest Gift of All." There were Mistletoe Bears followed yearly by the various Santa Bears. A different set of drinking mugs would be given out free to the customers in the Walnut Room if they purchased holiday drinks. The idea for these giveaway mugs first started as a promotion to "Irish Ways" in the Narcissus Room, when Field's highlighted all things Irish in the late 1970s. This promotion was a big hit, and it was moved to the Walnut Room, where it is still a Macy's tradition today.

Parker Brothers, maker of the board game Monopoly, made Marshall Field's its very own table board game. There were wonderful miniatures of the building and the clocks and many different styles of candy jars and candles. Recently, a replica of the clock was made into a small table lamp. The toy trucks that resembled the delivery trucks were my favorites. Margo and I remembered, come holiday time, all of the display windows surrounding the block and the way the store's interior would reflect the holiday spirit. These windows and interior displays were exciting to look forward to and were definitely a must-see. The main aisle had thick carpeting that extended the length of the first floor, and the four major platforms were decorated on both the north and south sides. These were always spectacular.

Year after year, interesting decorations were grouped together on these platforms. I can remember one year, Santa Claus on his sleigh arched over the main aisle with stringers of snowflakes cascading down from the ceiling in a fresh winter snowfall. Another year, there were different kinds of church steeples surrounded by snow and white trees. One year was especially nice. The display was called "The Seasons of Life—the Christmas remembering of 1979." There were four views of home life, one on each of the four platforms, with the characters growing older, emphasizing that time passes quickly and reminding us to enjoy life every day. One platform depicted children at play; another, a youth growing up; the third, a young adult maturing; and the last, seniors enjoying their family. All four displays were profoundly truthful.

All of these wonderful platforms and hand-made displays were created and crafted on the thirteenth floor in Field's own workshops, filled with carpenters and designers. To complete the effect, the first floor had some kind of garland streaming down from the ceiling and draped along the side walls. Stringers of snowflakes, holly, bright balls of color, beads and bows were all hand made by the great group of employees who made up the interior display department.

I would be remiss if I failed to mention just a few of the people who made these wonderful designs and decorations possible. First and foremost was the late Homer Sharp. Prior to working at Field's, he served our country in the United States Marine Corps with the Combat Intelligence Department. He came to Marshall Field's in 1946 after World War II and began as a window trimmer. He quickly rose through the ranks of the display department to the position of vice-president of design and soon became the resident historian and archivist. He was inducted into the National Association of Display Industries Hall of Fame in 1987. He stayed with Field's for forty-five years, doing what he loved: thinking up designs and having his talented staff follow them through to completion in Field's superior facilities. Under the guidance of Homer, these outstanding people made each year's Christmas season an experience filled with delight. He had a generous budget, and with his creative freedom, every year was spectacular. He was responsible for all the seasonal traditions: the Great Tree in the Walnut Room, the display windows and the store's interior decorations. Any holiday—be it the Fourth of July, with American flags flying everywhere, or Mother's Day, with a beautiful flower show in the springtime—was celebrated in splendor at Field's. It was Homer who had the foresight to save thousands of wonderful pictures going back as far as the 1800s, as well as the working scale models of the windows. He saved old invoices and receipts, menus and other significant memorabilia—like old hatboxes, kid gloves and even Marshall Field's roll-top desk and strongbox. This impressive collection of items since the store's first opening is now in the watchful hands of the Chicago History Museum.

Another outstanding individual was the late Annette Lewin, a longtime designer for the State Street store. Her main responsibility was to oversee, from concept to completion, the decorating and coordinating of the great forty-five-foot Walnut Room tree. She worked directly with Homer and the staff of the interior design department. She was a graduate of the Art Institute of Chicago. She worked for Field's thirty-one years and was another of those employees who gave every minute to her job with painstaking attention to detail. In addition to the tree, she designed Field's Crystal Palace Ice Cream Parlor in the 1970s. She also had the pleasant task of traveling to Europe several times to buy special ornaments for the tree-trimming shop.

Bob Starr, Virginia Paxton and Corleen Wald all headed up, in different years, the window display department. It was Homer Sharp who introduced these people, along with Johanna and Addis Osborne, to me. I had the great pleasure to listen to Bob and Virginia share their stories, as if I were a cub reporter taking in all of their recollections.

Tony Jahn followed Homer Sharp as archivist, and Amy Meadows became visual manager. They both kept the marvelous traditions going. To keep the concept of shock and awe, "fresh and effective" was their constant focus. It was an honor and a privilege to know all these people who worked their magic at Marshall Field's and made the slogan "Christmas isn't Christmas without a day at Field's" a wonderful truth.

During my research in the 1980s, I came across the following poem. It is simply titled "The Story of Uncle Mistletoe," by Helen McKenna. It was printed for the first time in my 2002 book, *Christmas on State Street: The 1940s and Beyond*, and I am proud to reprint it here with the permission of Macy's:

"The Story of Uncle Mistletoe"

In a mystical, magical land far away,
Where the moon lives by night and the sun lives by day,
Deep in the heart of the land called "Kerchoo,"
Not very far from the river Aldoo,
There lives in a house a most wonderful man,
I remember they call him, "the king of the land,"
You may have heard of him—maybe perchance?
I know just a word from him makes your heart dance!
You know him by name—Uncle Mistletoe's he,
A name that is known from the sea to the sea.

"But how did he come by that name?" you may ask,

"What did he do? What marvelous task?"
I tumbled these questions around in my mind,
I tumbled them forward, back, and behind,
At last I decided to go out and see,
To see what the answer he'd give me would be,
I knew where to look for him—surely no doubt!
There's one man that Misty is never without,
And that's with good reason, I found out, because
This one special man has the name Santa Claus.

I took to the air on the wings of a dream,
And landed by Santa there training his team,
I asked him about Uncle Mistletoe's name,
I asked him from where Uncle Mistletoe came,
He then sat me down on his knee and he smiled,
And asked, "Why are you such a curious child?"
I told him that I really wanted to know,
I told him, "I love Uncle Mistletoe so!"
He said, "Right up there is the river Aldoo,
And there Uncle Mistletoe's waiting for you."

And gosh! He was right! For I looked up ahead,
And there was the little man all dressed in red!
I knew by those sparkling eyes who he was,
(I cannot describe what a glimpse of them does!)
He said, "Ah! You're Billy that marvelous man,
Who asks all the questions I don't understand!"
"How do you know who I am?" I did cry,
"How do I know? Well because I am I!"
Then Santa stood up and he started to leave,
And he said, "Tell this boy of your first Christmas Eve!"

Uncle Mistletoe laughed with that laugh all his own,
And he said, "Long ago Santa Claus worked alone."
"No," I said, mystified, "That cannot be!"
"Santa has elves—Seven hundred and three!"

Marshall Field's and Christmas

He said, "Why do you never ask of the elves?"
"Where do you think that they come from themselves?"
"I do not know," I then said with a sigh,
"I don't understand and I can't even try!"
Uncle Mistletoe chuckled, "Well, come sit you down,
I'll tell you of when there was no Christmas town…"
"Santa had lived long ago by himself,
His only elf then was a toy on a shelf!
But people were growing in numbers each day,
The presents could not even fit on his sleigh.
Year after year he came through right on time,
Year after year every chimney he'd climb,
But with every step that old Santa would take,
His laughter would weaken—his sad heart would ache.
He knew that the next year there'd be even more,
And that was the Christmas of 1904!"

"Gee!" I exclaimed, "How did Santa survive?
How can that poor tired man be alive?"
"Listen, you'll know," Uncle Mistletoe said,
Beaming in warmth from his toes to his head.
"At the end of the Christmas of 1904,
Santa decided that he'd do no more;
'With no one to help me it's all I can do
To wrap up the gifts and deliver them too!
I'm hoping and praying that someone will hear,
And help me with Christmas time year after year!'

"And then in a flash, I appear to him there,
I told him I'd come in response to his prayer.
What I said to Santa to you I'll impart;
I am the spirit of Christmas that lives in your heart—
The spirit of living and kindness and love,
The spirit of giving that all men dream of—
Your Uncle in spirit and living in you,
And like mistletoe fresh and green when it's new
I symbolize all that your Christmas should be;
I'm the hope and the love that you always can see.

"And then in a flash I delivered the elves!
They filled up his pantries and closets and shelves!
The toys were so many we couldn't keep track!
(Elves, you see, always have had quite a knock
For helping out people who desperately need
Assistance in doing some good, kindly deed.)
They come from the world of Imagination,
Where Christmas is always a real celebration,
They live now with Santa—they built Christmas Town
With their kindness and love that they spread all around."

I must have been crying; he noticed a tear,
And he said, "Are you crying from laughter or fear?"
"Neither," said I, "I was crying because
There's so much to Christmas I never thought was!"
He said, "You thought that Christmas was only a season?
Then your celebration was for the wrong reason!"
"I see now!" I said, "Oh, I see it so clearly!
Christmas means giving to those you love dearly!"
"No," he said, "Christmas is never that small!
Christmas means giving—and giving to all!"

Giving to all? But what could I give?
What could I give to each person that lives?
I was going to ask him about what he said,
And the next thing I knew, I was home in my bed!
Now I was right back where I had begun,
I'd looked for the answer and I had found none.
But just then I saw something up by my books,
And I leaped from my bed so I might take a look.
There on the shelf was a little toy elf—
Holding a sign that said, "Give of yourself."

Giving of yourself—what a simple and marvelous thing to do! If all of us did just that, what a wonderful world it would be. As Christmases come and go, it is nice to remember the wonderful holiday spirit at Marshall Field's. There will never be the likes of a Marshall Field's again, with the true elegance, service and grandeur. One brick at a time…

5

CARSON, PIRIE, SCOTT & COMPANY

As mentioned earlier, the old Schlesinger and Mayer Store at State and Madison Streets was purchased by an ex-employee of Marshall Field's: Harry Gordon Selfridge. He in turn, as owner of the store, turned over the financial responsibility to Otto Young. All the while, Marshall Field retained title to the land itself, and it was bequeathed to the Field Museum upon his death. This network of businessmen, along with John Shedd, who was still associated with Field's as vice-president, was able to purchase the property from the sale of Selfridge's six thousand shares of Field's stockholdings.

I quote here, in part, my good friend, historian and archivist Ward Miller, who is an expert in all things Adler and Sullivan. Miller is executive director of the Richard Nickle Committee and coauthor, with Aaron Siskind, John Vinci and (the late) Richard Nickel, of the book *The Complete Architecture of Adler and Sullivan*:

> By 1904, Schlesinger & Mayer sold their store and building to Harry G. Selfridge, a former partner in Marshall Field and Company. Selfridge sold the business, known as H.G. Selfridge & Company a few months later to the retail concern of Carson, Pirie, Scott and Company, though the efforts of John G. Shedd, Levi Leiter, Otto Young and Marshall Field, who continued to own the land. It was a brokered deal, worked out in the rooms of the Illinois Trust Safe Deposit building, and based on several expensive land-leases and sub-leases and meant to further enhance the more affluent East side of State Street (thought to better serve the carriage trade arriving from the east, primarily Michigan Avenue and with access to these stores also on Wabash Avenue) with good competition which further benefited all the retailers and developers. Below is a written account of these negotiations by John G. Shedd, a former partner in the Marshall Field and Company Store:

"*Toward the end of July 1904, I had a call at my office from Mr. H. Gordon Selfridge, who, during the course of our conversation confided to me that on account of financial stress, which had not been fully anticipated by him, he found it necessary to make an arrangement that would alleviate this condition.*

"*He had accordingly made a verbal contract with Mr. Otto Young, then proprietor and manager of The Fair Stores* [located at the northwest corner of State and Adams Streets] *to sell him controlling interest in the business of H.G. Selfridge and Company, doing business at the southeast corner of Madison and State Streets, which business had been taken over by Mr. Selfridge as of June 11, 1904. Mr. Selfridge evidenced to me that this arrangement was not to his liking, but concluded it was good judgment to accept the conditions imposed by Mr. Young as it gave him the privilege of ultimately rebuying (within a certain number of years) control of the business which was then to be disposed of to Mr. Young, if he could make sufficient money out of the business to accomplish this result.*

"*As I was starting from our Retail Store* [Marshall Field and Company] *the following morning about eleven o'clock, I chanced to meet Mr. John T. Pirie, head of the house of Carson Pirie Scott & Company, who apologetically said he was looking around just to see how we were doing things.*

"*Having in mind the attitude of Mr. Selfridge and the knowledge that the store then occupied by Carson Pirie Scott & Company at the southwest corner of State and Washington* [the Reliance Building, now also known as the Hotel Burnham] *had been sold to Hillmans* [a grocery concern] *and consequently they had for some months been seeking a new location without success, it occurred to me as a friendly act that I might negotiate between Mr. Pirie and Mr. Selfridge the sale of the Selfridge store to Carson Pirie Scott & Company. I accordingly invited Mr. Pirie to my office on the fifth floor of our Retail building. He demurred for some time, but upon my intimation that I had something I wanted to point out to him he accompanied me.*

"*The conversation that followed was relative to the possibility of his buying or arranging with Mr.* [Marshall] *Field to buy and build a proper store for the occupancy of Carson Pirie Scott & Company at a location comprising the southwest corner of Randolph and State Streets* [the Springer and Kranz Blocks, also known as the Bay State Building—now part of Block 37] *including the Borden property, the then owner of which relied very largely upon Mr. Field for advice as to its disposition. Mr. Pirie protested this was not possible for two reasons. First he did not think Mr. Field would do it—secondly, it was a larger responsibility than he cared to incur. His reason for thinking Mr. Field would not do it was that he thought Mr. Field bore some feeling of resentment toward their concern on account of a former transaction in which Field Leiter & Company* [later called Marshall Field and Company] *had to* *pay them a bonus of $100,000 for the so-called Singer Building.* [This structure became the retail store of Marshall Field and Company, located at the northeast corner of Washington and State Streets.] *I assured Mr. Pirie that was positively not the case and that Mr. Field had no feeling of antagonism toward any man for his success in any straight forward bargain, which might go against him.*

"I then stated if the proposition was agreeable from his point of view, I believed he could buy out Mr. Selfridge. He assured me that the matter had been exhausted and he would not care to take it up, but upon my assurance that being a friend of both I believed it might be possible to bring them together, and armed as I was with the knowledge imparted to me by Mr. Selfridge the previous evening, I convinced Mr. Pirie that if he would allow me to negotiate as a friend of both I would undertake the matter immediately. I asked him to call his son Sam C. Pirie to the phone and impart to him the knowledge that I had made the proffer and it was necessary to meet immediately if anything was to be done. Within a half hour, it was arranged that Mr. Selfridge and Mr. Sam C. Pirie should meet me immediately in the consultation rooms of the Illinois Trust Safe Deposit Company.

"I secured three rooms, occupying the center room myself, Mr. Selfridge the one on the right, Mr. Pirie the one on the left, and opened up the question as to the possibilities. Within possibly a half hour's time, I had arranged with Mr. Selfridge that on condition of Carson Pirie Scott accepting the business of Selfridge & Company as of June 11, 1904 (the date of his purchase) that he would sell the property to them for a bonus of $250,000. Mr. Pirie immediately offered $150,000. These figures I noted on a scrap of paper, and after some negotiations they compromised on $200,000 as it appears on the slip…Mr. Sam C. Pirie simply writing 'Sold S.C.P.' and I having full authority wrote 'O.K. Selfridge,' and then called Mr. Selfridge and Mr. Pirie together.

"Mr. Selfridge and Mr. Pirie acknowledged consummation of the contract except that Mr. Selfridge not having advised Mr. [Otto] *Young of what he desired to do, and feeling under some restraint on account of the possibility of Mr. Young taking the position that his tentative arrangement with him, which was only verbal, might be insisted upon, Mr. Selfridge wrote on one corner of the slip 'O.K. if Young agrees.'*

"The next morning Mr. Young having agreed with Mr. Selfridge to relinquish his claim, Mr. Selfridge asked for an appointment to complete the terms of the contract. However, Mr. Sam Pirie telephoned Mr. Selfridge that his partners were not quite satisfied with the transaction and desired to open it up for further consideration, and Mr. Selfridge telephoned asking my advice. I told him I thought the matter was concluded, but if there was any question we had better have another meeting, which was arranged for ten o'clock that morning, Mr. Selfridge occupying the same room as the day before, and Mr. Pirie, Sr., Mr. George Scott, Mr. Robert Scott, Mr.

[Andrew] *MacLeish and Mr. Sam C. Pirie appearing for Carson Pirie Scott &
Company occupying the other rooms.*

*"The partners debated the matter with me for two hours, and finally it being
evident that it was the only opportunity for Carson Pirie Scott & Company to
continue retail business on State Street, and my person urging them to take this
opportunity of securing for themselves a location on one of the best retail business
corners in the world, they finally proposed a compromise, agreeing to take over the
business of Selfridge & Company as of June 11, 1904, assuming all responsibility
of the Selfridge regime and paying Mr. Selfridge a bonus of $150,000 which Mr.
Selfridge instructed me to accept.*

*"I then brought them together in my room and after congratulations all around
and many profuse expressions of admiration from Mr. John T. Pirie to me for my
helpfulness in saving their institution for the Street, appointments were made with
counsel and the contract consummated.*

"I make this statement so that a record of the transaction will be preserved."

Even before German immigrants Leopold Schlesinger and David Mayer acquired
the Carson, Pirie, Scott Building (now the Sullivan Center), it was the former Bowen
Building, designed by William W. Boyington in 1872.

It was said that after Harry Selfridge left employment at Field's after twenty-five
years of loyal service, "old boss man" Field remarked, "We'll have to get another
office boy." Selfridge was admired for his brilliant ideas. He was known as the "go-
to point person." The Selfridge department store in this building was brief. He sold
to new buyers: Sam Carson, John T. Pirie and new partner Robert Scott. They had
a store on Lake Street but believed relocating to State Street would be in their best
interests. Even though they would be much nearer to their top competitor, Marshall
Field's, they felt it would be more appealing to shoppers to have a choice of where
to make their purchases. And the foot traffic, encouraging window-shopping, would
increase sales.

Immigrants from Northern Ireland, both Samuel Carson and his best boyhood
friend, John T. Pirie, had slight setbacks in coming to America. They booked passage
aboard the *Philadelphia*. Unfortunately, it was shipwrecked off Newfoundland. They
were detained slightly and eventually ended up in New York. They soon came west
to the railroad town of Amboy, Illinois, where they stayed for four years, opening a
dry goods store in 1854. Slowly at first, they watched the business grow. The store's
reputation grew, and new locations opened in towns like Mendota, Polo, Galena and
Sterling, making Carson's the first group of chain stores in Illinois. They opened their
first Chicago store in 1864, near State and Lake Streets.

The Carson, Pirie, Scott stairway and railings reflected Sullivan's design throughout the store. This was the first floor, looking down toward the basement. *Photo © Robert P. Ledermann.*

Carson had secured enough money to send for and sponsor his bride-to-be and best friend's sister, Elizabeth Pirie, from Belfast, Ireland. Still another best friend, Robert Scott, came to America and quickly became a partner with Carson and Pirie. The three men formed the partnership of Carson, Pirie, Scott in 1890. They moved into the State and Madison Streets building in 1904.

The architect Louis H. Sullivan's building was the partnership's flagship store. It was a showcase structure with spectacular ornamental ironwork surrounding the entrance and rotunda, with swirls and intricate lines of grillwork, steel-frame construction and gleaming white terra cotta tile trim. Years passed, and a twelve-story addition was constructed by Daniel Burnham. Another was added in 1927 by Burnham Bros., and in 1960, the Holabird and Root architectural firm built yet another addition. Nine floors complemented the original store. This location—One South State Street—was prime and soon became known as the world's busiest corner. The interior of the building reflected Sullivan's ornamental ironwork, with ornate details on the railings and balusters, as well as in the trim on the stair risers and undersides, on the decorative screens of all the elevators and on the radiators against the wall that sent heat through the floors. Even the interior columns and capitals that touched the ceilings were topped off and surrounded with that marvelous, unmistakable Sullivan signature ironwork. If you should ever be passing by outside the entrance, stop and try to find the hidden monograms "S&M" and "LHS." These monograms belong to the owners, Schlesinger and Mayer, and Louis H. Sullivan. They are inscribed within the ironwork.

To say the Chicago fire of 1871 was a blessing in disguise would not be kind, but Chicago after the fire became a key location for new commerce, transportation and rebirth, drawing engineers and marvelous architects like Daniel Hudson Burnham,

Holidays on State Street (2004): A Time Honored Tradition. Anchoring the corner of State and Madison Streets is the Carson, Pirie, Scott Building, designed by famed architect Louis Henry Sullivan. This department store was at this historic location from 1904 to 2007. This watercolor painting is by Jack Simmerling. *Print used with permission of John J. (Jack) Simmerling/The Heritage Gallery, Ltd.*

Frank Lloyd Wright and our extraordinary Louis H. Sullivan. As a side note, Sullivan and his wife, Margaret Hattabough, lived at one time at 4575 Lake Park Avenue in the Kenwood neighborhood of Chicago.

Even as he was designing the rotunda, Sullivan knew it would be another "extra" to highlight the building, along with the unique ironwork. Upon entering the store, with its walnut paneling around the airy vestibule, one gets a feeling of grandeur that truly sets the building apart. Over the years, Carson's realized it could decorate the outside of the rotunda or advertise a store's theme during the holiday season. One year, it had a huge Nutcracker, standing tall like a beacon, on guard along State Street. This helped to alert passing pedestrians that the decorative Christmas windows that year depicted the story of the Nutcracker. Still another year—1977—had larger-than-life figures from the Charles Dickens classic story "A Christmas Carol." A very tall Bob Cratchet, with Tiny Tim on his shoulders, was on top of the rotunda with the windows reflecting the story, complete with Scrooge and all the ghosts. Most years, Carson's gift to Chicago was the traditional wood-carved Nativity set, with the Holy family, wise men and shepherds.

Perhaps the quote in my previously written book by famed *Tribune* architectural critic Blair Kamin said it best:

> *No State Street department store, not even Marshall Field's, is more important in the history of architecture. The Carson, Pirie, Scott, and Company store was one of Louis Sullivan's greatest designs, perhaps his greatest, an epoch-defining image that transformed the static rationality of its structural steel frame into a superbly fluid composition that welcomes the shoppers with an intricate veil of cast iron ornament.*

I am still inclined to agree with him.

The words "Rules to Employees" were on a plaque I recently stumbled upon. I dare say they would not be welcomed in any retail workplace of today. Nonetheless, it an amusing read. The date on the plaque was 1856, and it must have been used by Carson's at the beginning of its dry goods retail business in Amboy, Illinois.

Carson, Pirie, Scott, and Company
----Rules to Employees----

Store must be open from 6 a.m. to 9 p.m.

Store must be swept, counters and chimneys cleaned, a pail of water, also a bucket of coal brought in before breakfast, and attend to customers who will call.

Store must not be open on the Sabbath Day unless necessary and then only for a few minutes.

The employee, who is in the habit of smoking Spanish cigars, being shaved at the barber shop, going to dances and other places of amusement, will surely give his employer reason to be suspicious of his honesty and integrity.

Each employee must not pay less than $5.00 per year to the church and must attend Sunday School regularly.

Men employees are given one evening a week for courting and two if they go to prayer meeting.

After 14 hours of work in the store, the leisure time should be spent mostly in reading.
Signed: "The Management"

These rules and regulations are laughable today, of course.

After the fire, Carson's focused on plush comforts in the customers' waiting room. Considerable attention toward privacy, ventilation and lighting—with spacious chairs, ornamentation and embellishment—made the customer more relaxed. However, it was said that these "comforts" were for the exclusive use of Carson's customers and that if any employee were to be found using them, he or she would probably be discharged. It was clearly understood these rest areas were reserved for Carson's patrons.

Carson's had some of the same customer services Field's had. They both had pedestrian walkway bridges high across Wabash Avenue that took the customer directly to the elevated trains. They believed the customers deserved the most courteous and attentive service—that superior customer satisfaction was their number one priority. They trained their employees and associates to be readily available to provide convenient service.

Carson, Pirie, Scott kept up the responsibilities of stewardship of the State Street store. It was somewhat confusing and involved, but the men's diligence paid off. They leased the building until 1955, when they finally had the opportunity to purchase it as their flagship store, after some sixty-five years, from the Otto Young estate. In 1978, they finally bought the land on which the building stands from the Field Museum of Natural History. Throughout the years, the store has had many additions, restorations and remodelings, and in 1959, the structure was designated a Chicago landmark, reaffirmed again in 1970. Finally, that same year, this beautiful Sullivan-designed building was added to the National Registry of Historical Places. And in 1975, the National Historical Landmarks Program added the Carson, Pirie, Scott Building to its prestigious listing.

In 1999, the *Sun Times* printed an interesting article by staff reporter Mark Shectic. He was comparing the prices people in Chicago had to pay for items back in 1899 to what they were paying one hundred years later. He selected a few categories we all can relate to. In entertainment, a ticket to the Chicago Symphony for a Saturday night performance would range from sixty cents to $1.50. In 1999, the prices ranged from $23.00 up to $175.00 per ticket. Transportation was still a premium. A horse and buggy purchase in 1889 would cost $150.00, but for a luxury car in 1993, you would spend upwards of $32,000.00. A pair of women's top-of-the-line shoes back then were $2.98; in 1999, they cost $300.00. In 1899, one pound of coffee was twenty-eight cents, and five pounds of sugar was twenty-five cents. In 1999, you could expect to pay $5.98 for a pound of coffee and ninety-nine cents for a pound of sugar.

Carson, Pirie, Scott was no Marshall Field's—"the crown jewel" of department stores on State Street—but it could hold its head high with the best of them. Its prices were

In the 1960s, Carson's honored the servicemen of our country with a minute of silence throughout the store. *Courtesy of* Chicago Sun-Times *Newspaper Media/Archival Department.*

set in the moderate to slightly higher price range. The friendly rivalry on State Street between Marshal Field's and Carson's would last for years. They would constantly try to entice shoppers into their stores. Sure, Field's had many specialty departments, but then Carson's did, too. Just like Field's, Carson's had buses that carried suburbanites from various train stations back and forth to the store. In later years, Amling's Flower World Shop would welcome shoppers on the first floor. Carson's Budget store on the lower level was remodeled. A Tartan Tray Cafeteria and the Honey Bear Shop, which was connected with the Honey Bear Farm complex off Powers Lake, also moved in.

In appreciation, Carson, Pirie, Scott wrote a letter of recommendation for Sullivan in 1906 about its new store. The following quote is taken from the Sullivan Centennial file in the museum archives at the Art Institute of Chicago:

The high taste and skill of Mr. Louis H. Sullivan, its architect, are all expressed in the beautiful designs and general style of this structure, and our occupancy of it for these two years enables us to form an intelligent judgment upon its excellence as a structure as well as its adaptations for retail mercantile purposes. No more beautiful corner entrance of its kind is, so far as we know, in existence in this country; and the whole is a fine illustration of what Mr. Sullivan can design in the way of a retail business building. We learn from Messrs. Schlesinger and Mayer that their transactions with Mr. Sullivan were perfectly satisfactory, and gladly add our words of approval to his skill and success as an architect.

The years of expanding, modifications and restorations did not compromise Sullivan's original designs. With every upgrade to the building, Carson's would run newspaper ads announcing the changes throughout the store. It explained that with every reopening, it was thoroughly confident that it would continue to meet the high expectations of its customers.

Carson's also had afternoon tea, served daily from 3:00 until 5:00 p.m. in the Tea Room. A separate "men's grill" welcomed smoking. This men's restaurant was on the eighth floor, Wabash side. There were reading, writing and waiting rooms with a bank of telephone booths nearby.

Carson's Heather House Restaurant was opened in September 1959. The space had previously been occupied by two former restaurants. The Maypool and Georgian Rooms together had a seating capacity of five hundred. I remember fondly that the highlight of the Heather House was the fifty-foot hand-painted panoramic mural of Edinburgh, Scotland, in 1880, with its soft green and beige tones. This was created by A.R. Gordon in 1959. In the center was the Scotts Monument and to the right was the hilltop with Edinburgh Castle. The remaining side walls, as well as a huge screen partition, had pressed Heather sprigs embedded into the frosted panes of Lucite. At lunchtime, the specialty was the legendary buffet with its famous, freshly baked sticky cinnamon buns. Carson's boasted that it had the biggest salad bar in town. It had fashion shows going on while the customers lunched, displaying the new designers featured in the store. This charming restaurant was closed in May 1988 and was demolished in 1989 to make room for an upscale computer room. In later years, it was changed again into an employee lunchroom.

It was tradition each year for Carson's to have large banners flanking each interior doorway that counted down the number of days until Christmas. Upon entering the first floor of Carson's during the holidays, you received an eye-opening surprise. Each of the supporting columns, as far as your eye could see, was decorated with seasonal designs—usually wrapped with colorful foil paper and then elaborated with lots of extra garlands, beads, berries, holly

Postcard of Carson's Heather House Restaurant on the eighth floor, with the mural of Edinburgh, Scotland, surrounding the main back wall. *Robert P. Ledermann, private collection.*

and snowflakes. This same motif was carried over to the chandeliers and looped back to the columns. To greet Christmas shoppers (sometimes but not always), Carson's rolled out its plush red carpet as well. And speaking of red carpets, when a celebrity was in town to promote a book, play, movie or product, you were sure to see him or her on Carson's third floor, behind a fantastic French writing desk, with the huge sparkling-clean rotunda windows looking onto State and Madison Streets as a backdrop. The celebrity would sit and sign autographs for fans. Carson's also utilized its auditorium on the eighth floor for such occasions. The auditorium was between the Heather House Restaurant and the men's grill. This was a huge, brightly lit room with a stage, and during the holidays you could find Santa Claus sitting on a throne with elaborate woodcarvings, waiting to greet his admirers. I can remember entering through a set of double doors in the back, visiting Santa and getting a little paper-and-mesh Christmas stocking or a coloring book, then exiting through another set of double doors in the back. Walking to the auditorium, you had to pass through the hallway where Carson's hung publicity pictures of some of the visiting celebrities throughout the years.

The trim-a-tree department was spectacular, offering everything you needed for a tree trimming and more: greeting cards; wrapping paper; ribbons; tags; bows; ornaments of every color, size and shape; and garland to match. The area was twinkling with glitter and lights. Any color or size Christmas tree and lights were

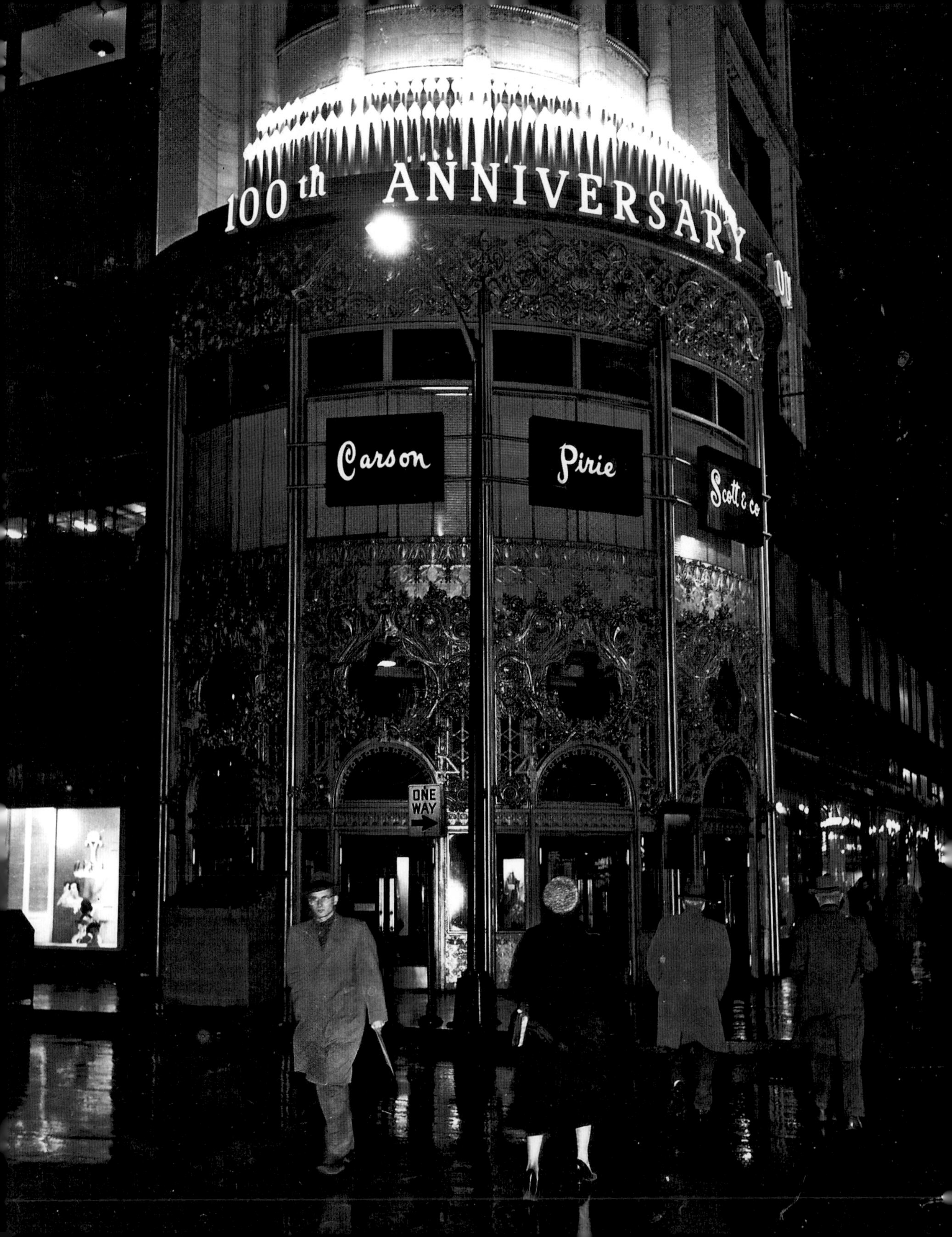
100th ANNIVERSARY
Carson
Pirie
Scott & co
ONE WAY

Above: Empty shelves and bare floors and walls on Carson's second floor on March 16, 2007. There was only sunshine streaming through the signature windows that overlook State and Madison Streets. It was a sad walk for me that day. *Photo © Robert P. Ledermann.*

Opposite: Carson's celebrated one hundred years in business, from 1854 to 1954, by placing one hundred lights resembling candles on top of the rotunda. *Courtesy of* Chicago Sun-Times *Newspaper Media/Archival Department.*

available, along with novelties, candles, stocking stuffers, tree skirts and stockings to hang by the chimney with care. Carson's always had an extensive selection of Studio 56–themed houses and side accessories to match.

To look back and remember the Carson, Pirie, Scott store on State Street was a warm feeling for me. As a child going to the department store, and then as an adult working in the Loop, I always thought that State Street, Field's and Carson's were permanent—the standard of stability—and shopping would always be there. I'm sure that's what Carson's thought, too, when it celebrated its 100th anniversary. At the Carson, Pirie, Scott & Co.'s 100th anniversary dinner, on January 20, 1954, the who's who of retail was all there at the head tables. One of the television personalities at that time, Herb Shriner, came to Chicago to entertain them. The guests were similar to those at a neighborhood block party—everyone knew who lived at the big house up the block. Besides the Carson, Pirie and Scott families, there were Mr. and Mrs.

Clearing out all memories at Carson's State Street store. *Photo © Robert P. Ledermann.*

Joel Goldblatt, the W.W. Kohl family, the David Mayer family, Mr. and Mrs. Hughston McBain and Elmer T. Stevens, as well as some of Marshall Field's family. At night, the rotunda had one hundred lights resembling candles on top, sparkling in the night sky, advertising the store's accomplishment of one hundred years in retail. Sadly, everything must have an ending.

P.A. Bergner purchased Carson's under a subsidiary of a Swiss company. The store went through a series of ownership, including Proffitts, Inc. (later renamed Saks, Inc.) and Bon-Ton Stores, Inc., all the while retaining the name Carson, Pirie, Scott & Company. Carson's still maintained stores in the surrounding suburbs of Chicago and throughout the Midwest area. Bankruptcy is a nasty business, and Carson's emerged briefly. Its branch stores were doing well, but in Chicago in the late 1970s, the population was moving out of the city and into the suburbs, and Carson's State Street sales were dwindling. It was decided that the State Street flagship store would close its doors for good on February 21, 2007. The building needed major repairs, both on the interior and exterior. The windows needed to be reset and reglazed. The flooring, walls and lighting all needed to be attended to. The Art Institute of Chicago and part of the School of the Art Institute now occupies several floors. The 600,000-square-foot building complex has been renamed the Sullivan Center, and all the cast-iron grillwork covering the entrance of Sullivan's building was dismantled, cleaned, corrected and put back in place as originally intended.

Ward Miller has been gracious enough to offer few additional remarks:

In response to the expansion of the new buildings of the Marshall Field & Company store, designed by D.H. Burnham, dating from 1902 and 1906 and perhaps the addition of two new large 7½-ton bronze clocks at State and Randolph and State and Washington Streets, to replace a former clock on that site dating to 1892, a clock was designed for Carson Pirie Scott.

Above, left: Even the escalators in Carson's have stopped running. This view looks down from the forth floor to the third. *Photo © Robert P. Ledermann.*

Above, right: Looking through the "Pirie" window of Carson's onto State Street and Block 37 under construction in 2007. *Photo © Robert P. Ledermann*

The origins of the clock are not known, since paperwork has not been located to further the story. However, the two possible designs reflect the style and creativity of Louis Sullivan and are stamped by the Winslow Brothers, known for their superb ornamental castings and their work on the building with Louis Sullivan.

The larger clock would have extended outward from above the center entrance to the store at State and Madison Streets, like a tree growing out from the side of a river embankment—a very naturalistic form, much in keeping with Sullivan's ornamental designs. The clock as drawn in this sketch would have extended upward twenty feet in the air, engaging into the ornamental fascia and cornice of the cast iron façade of the lower floors, would have bracketed out more than ten feet from the building. This

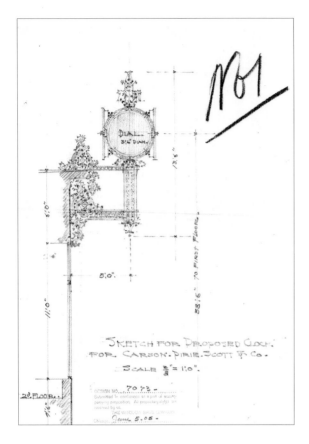

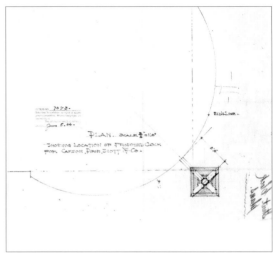

Above: Photo of the blueprint showing the location of where the proposed clock would have been mounted on the 1906 exterior of Carson's at State and Madison Streets. *Courtesy of Ward Miller and the Richard Nickel Committee, in honor of Martha Ward Miller.*

Left: One of Carson's hidden blueprint sketches of the clock (that never came to be). *Courtesy of Ward Miller and the Richard Nickel Committee, in honor of Martha Ward Miller.*

organic design which would have been original in its approach was apparently not the favored solution of the two schemes, since the smaller variation, measuring thirteen and a half feet was further developed with a title block and more notations. This smaller scheme would have been placed higher on the building, about the location of the fascia and cornice of the ornamental cast iron and extending upward and interfacing with the cream-colored terra cotta plane of the third floor. Either of these solutions may have been considered and it is not known the extent of Louis Sullivan's involvement in these designs at this time. However, the originality of the designs cannot be denied.

Recently, a wonderful thing happened—to the delight of Sullivan and Carson, Pirie, Scott history fans. Ward Miller, executive director of the Richard Nickel Committee, had the fortune to obtain a few boxes of miscellaneous Carson's memorabilia. Among this memorabilia were original sketches of clocks that Sullivan may have wanted to use for Carson's on State Street, similar to the Field's clocks. *Chicago Tribune* architectural

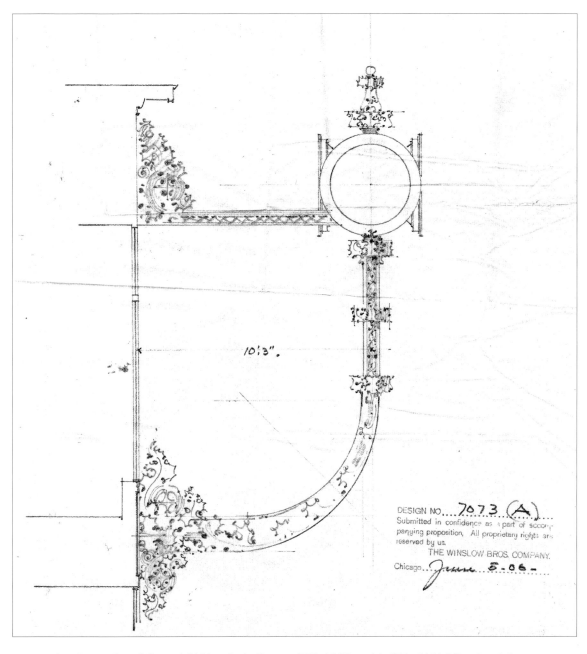

10'3".

Another version of Carson's hidden clock. *Courtesy of Ward Miller and the Richard Nickel Committee, in honor of Martha Ward Miller.*

columnist Blair Kamin wrote an article about this discovery entitled "The Mystery of the Big Carson's Clock That Never Was." It read, in part, "The finding shocked him, just as it would stun anyone who has grown accustomed to the geometric purity of the store's cylinder-shaped rotunda." It was my good fortune to meet with Miller and to be graced with permission to use these sketches in my book. This is the first time these hidden Carson, Pirie, Scott sketches have appeared in print.

It was reported that the newest renovation budget was $68.9 million, undertaken by the real estate redevelopment firm Joseph Freed and Associates, LLC. This firm, along with Target, announced on February 15, 2011, that the Target Corporation would lease approximately 125,000 square feet spread over the first two floors of the building. Most of the space would be used for selling apartment essentials, trendy clothing and fresh foods. The State Street demographics have changed with the times. The student population in nearby dormitories will surely benefit from its new neighbor. One brick at a time…

6

OTHER NEIGHBORS

If State Street could talk, what stories would it tell? Up through the 1980s, State Street still had the excitement and glamour that it was known for, but things were beginning to lose their luster. Close your eyes and let your mind drift back to the memories of your childhood, adolescence or adulthood. Think back to happier times—your junior or senior prom; a special date with that person you so wanted to impress; perhaps a shopping trip to find a good topcoat to keep you warm on Chicago's cold winter days. Maybe you were looking for an expensive wedding gift or a new pair of well-fitting shoes. Where did you go to see the latest movie? What was your favorite movie theater? After the movie—or even before—did you have a little lunch or dinner, or maybe a soda or malt? And how did you get there? No car? No problem. You were in good company. Like a lot of people, you probably took public transportation: a train, a bus or two, the subway, the old-fashioned streetcars or the el (short for the elevated trains that run on elevated tracks surrounding the Loop). "The Loop" was an affectionate nickname pedestrians and commuters gave to the main streets of Chicago—from Lake Street to the north, Van Buren to the south, Wabash to the east and Wells to the west—when the horse-drawn cable cars and buggies would loop back and forth from train stations and businesses. And it stuck.

The subway provided faster and more direct access to State Street from the neighborhoods when it was completed and opened in 1943. In earlier years, the streetcars—or the "trolley"—would travel to the center of State Street. You waited on an island in the middle of the street or walked up to the streetcar from the curb. Boarding was at the back of the streetcar, where you paid your fare to a uniformed conductor, who encouraged you to move upward into the car to find a seat. The

motorman would be in his own partitioned area and would recognize that when you pulled the cord above the seat, you were signaling to get off at the next stop.

Whether walking up and down State Street enjoying the old-fashioned hobby of window shopping or checking the prices of things you might want to purchase, going downtown was the place to do it. People would take care of how they were dressed. Ladies wore hats and gloves and most of the time a nice dress or suit. Men wore dress suits, and children would wear their Sunday best: good shoes, trousers, pretty dresses and caps or hats. Blue jeans and T-shirts were just not seen. Even cab and bus drivers and train personnel would work in proper uniforms and hats. People used to take pride in themselves, and it showed in their manner and the way they dressed when they were on State Street.

All the names up and down State Street fall back into place in my mind with an ease and fondness that brings a smile to my face. The department stores alone were truly a shopper's delight. Besides her two royal majesties—Marshall Field's (now Macy's) and Carson, Pirie, Scott & Company (now the Sullivan Center, with Target soon to move into the first and second floors)—there was The Fair, Montgomery Ward, Goldblatts (previously the Davis Store), Sears and Roebuck, Mandle Brothers (Wieboldt's) and the Boston Store. The ladies' and men's clothing specialty stores were Stevens, Baskins, Benson/Rixons (the store's slogan was "The best ads aren't written, they are worn"), Rothschilds, Bonds, Lyttons ("The Lytton Look") and Karoll's (the Red Hanger men's shop). And don't forget all the shoe stores: Maylings, Chandler's, Bakers and O.G.'s (O'Connor and Goldberg's). My wife has fond memories of the giant windows with all the shoes on display ("eye candy" in today's terminology).

The movie theaters played a huge role in our lives—spectacular movie palaces that took you to a different world of elegance, each more elaborate than the last. The Roosevelt at 110 North State Street, the State and Lake at 190 North State and the Little Loop next to the last remaining and still active grand lady, the Chicago Theater, on the east side of State Street at 175 North State Street, were other theaters on or very near State Street. There was also the United Artists, the Michael Todd, the McVickers, the Monroe, the Woods, the Oriental and the Randolph. Some had grand lobbies, plush carpeting, marble columns, indirect decorative lighting, mezzanines,

Corner of State and Randolph Streets in front of Marshall Field's State Street store, November 23, 1947. Linda Graves and her father, Austin Graves, vice-president for the store in Chicago at the time, planted Moline elm trees. It is interesting to note that the famed striped window (to the right) was one of a set of windows for that Christmas season when Field's repeated the story "A Christmas Dream" with the popular Uncle Mistletoe. *Courtesy of* Chicago Sun-Times *Newspaper Media/Archival Department.*

carved plastered ceilings with gold gilding or colorful paint, orchestra pits, balconies and spacious seats. The Mighty Wurlitzer Organ is still at the Chicago Theater.

Prior to showing Hollywood movies, these movie houses were involved with vaudeville, live stage shows, burlesque, dance interpretations, music, comedians, minstrel shows and voluptuous showgirls. Burlesque queens Gypsy Rose Lee and Sally Rand—scantily dressed striptease artists whose acts involved partial or total nudity—were part of the history of these movie houses. Popular artists throughout these years came to Chicago to try out their acts before going on to New York or touring the country. Al Jolson, Sophie Tucker, Danny Kaye, Bob Hope, Dean Martin, Jerry Lewis, Frank Sinatra, Kate Smith, Bing Cosby, Red Skelton, Rosemary Clooney and Jack Benny all appeared at these theaters at one time or another. In later years, rock 'n' roll, jazz bands and popular singing stars graced the stages. The entertainment in the theaters went from live shows to silent black-and-white films. These oldies but goodies had captions and were shown with live organ accompaniment. Not long after this, talking movies were introduced. Although it was a slow change for these movie houses to show more "talkies," the movie studios were opening and producing more talking films than silent films, and the industry continued in this direction.

Barney Balaban's humble beginnings in Chicago started in 1908. His family were Russian Jews, and he grew up in the Maxwell Street neighborhood where they had a grocery store. His family owned a small theater on the near west side and ran every aspect of the business, from the box office to running the films. It grew into the city's largest movie theater chain, known as the Balaban and Katz Theaters. Then his family built another movie house, the Circle Theater. By 1915, Balaban had teamed up with his soon-to-be partner Sam Katz, another entrepreneur who had big plans to build a deluxe movie palace. This was the Central Park. They were on their way. Barney was quoted as saying:

> *We orthodox Jews have a duty to perform, an obligation to pay. In the early period of Jewish immigration most of our people came here poor and destitute. Now that many of us possess wealth, it is time we take up the responsibility ourselves, to build and maintain the charitable and philanthropic institutions and to create such others as modern American Jews may require.*

His success is reflected in the movie houses he built, each one more extravagant than the last: the Riviera (modeled after the chapel of Versailles), the Granada, the Century and Chicago's State Street grand ladies—the State and Lake, the Roosevelt and, in 1921, the Chicago Theater (still in business today). The Chicago Theater is mainly a concert venue hosting singing stars, recording bands and comedians, but it is also rented out for parties or commercial events.

Crowds near Monroe on State Street in 1959. *Courtesy of* Chicago Sun-Times *Newspaper Media/ Archival Department.*

Wonderful history is on the walls of the stairwells and halls and on the backstage doors, as well as on both sides of the stage in the Chicago Theater. The signatures, poems, artwork, words of wisdom, vignettes and more than ten thousand autographs cover over three floors of the building. Frank Sinatra started this tradition on September 14, 1986, writing, "Having a super time, I just did." And many performers followed, including Bill Cosby, Roy Orbison, Tom Dreesen, Sammy Davis Jr., Liza Minnelli, Dean Martin, Lauryn Hill and Carlos Morel, to name a few.

Still, Chicago had a reputation for its shadier side, maintaining a group of movie theaters that put up with dancing showgirls and strippers. These were mainly on South State Street: the Alhambra, the American, the Folly Theater, (later known as the State-Congress), the Gem, the Orpheum, the Rialto and the Trocadero.

It's interesting that you can travel the world and strike up a conversation with a total stranger, only to discover that you are both from Chicago. You instantly become friends, and your conversation carries on and on. You stir up nostalgic experiences. You bring up your favorite haunts, both existing and long gone. Perhaps you met your spouse on one New Years' Eve celebration at State and Madison Streets. Maybe you recall the excitement of your first parade, standing at the curb for hours, waiting to see—in person—celebrities, political candidates, astronauts, cowboy heroes or even a president-to-be.

In August 1927, Charles A. Lindbergh came to town, shortly after his historic New York–Paris flight in the *Spirit of St. Louis*. It was said that thousands lined the route along State Street and threw torn telephone book confetti at his black limousine. Franklin D. Roosevelt rode down the street in the early stages of his first term as president of the United States. Millions saw him again when he came in October 1937 to open a State Street bridge. After World War II, Dwight D. Eisenhower rode in a parade. In 1951, General Douglas MacArthur rode in a convertible in another parade with Mayor Martin H. Kennelly. President Harry Truman visited Chicago for the parade in 1952 and again in 1956.

Your feet were throbbing by the time you got home, but it was worth it. Before, during and after the parade, you saw Chicago's "finest": the police department in their uniforms, doing what they love best, providing comfort and safety to the public. Sometimes they were in their squad cars; sometimes they were riding in their three-wheeler motor buggies or standing guard in the middle of the streets directing traffic or even seen riding on top of an impressive horse.

You and your new friend play a little catch-up about what's happening in Chicago, what store went out of business and who moved in. You mention some little-known trivia, like the fact that George M. Pullman moved to Chicago and started to experiment on his model of the perfect railroad car there. It was a success, with beautifully frescoed woodwork, fine upholstered chairs and rich carpets. His prototype was named the Pioneer. It was honored when it carried President Abraham Lincoln's precious remains to Chicago and then on to Springfield, Illinois—his final resting place.

The Goldblatt family emigrated from Poland and at first ran a grocery and butcher shop in a Chicago west side neighborhood in the early 1900s. As luck would have it, during the Great Depression, the family did exceedingly well, expanding and purchasing several additional department stores throughout Chicago's neighborhoods. By 1936, the Goldblatt brothers—Maurice, Nathan, Joel and Louis—had acquired the former Davis Store at Van Buren and State Streets. They had stores as early as 1933 in nearby Joliet, Illinois, and Hammond, Indiana, with the company's annual sales exceeding $20 million. The funny thing about these wonderful vintage buildings up and down State Street is that they remain, perhaps being remodeled a bit, but the names get changed. This was the case for this Davis Store building. Back in 1923, the building had belonged to A.M. Rothschild. Then, Marshall Field acquired it and renamed it the Davis Store, until he sold it in 1936 to the Goldblatt family.

In the Chicago neighborhoods, the immigrant families were loyal to the local department stores. Most of the time, they continued to frequent the neighborhood chain department stores as opposed to traveling downtown to the larger State Street department stores. With the flagship store on State Street, along with some forty-five additional branch or neighborhood locations, the Goldblatt retail family peaked with close to $250 million in annual sales in the mid-1970s, with eight thousand employees and staff.

In the late 1970s, newcomers to the retail field started dotting the neighborhoods and suburbs. Companies like Kmart, Woolworth's, Zayre and Shopper's World were called discount chains. These stores were difficult competition for the consumers' dollars. Middle-class shoppers were no longer enticed to shop at Goldblatt's but could use their hard-earned dollars at new discount stores and get good bargains. Amidst increased competition and changing markets, Goldblatt's filed for bankruptcy. It emerged out of financial debt briefly, only to sell the business, with the remaining six neighborhood stores, to J.G. Industries, Inc., in 1985. The remaining stores stayed opened, still under the Goldblatt name, until 2003, when they went out of business and were liquidated.

The flagship store at 333 South State Street was purchased by DePaul University. Even today, signs of the past still live on. Look up at the façade of smooth terra cotta tiles on the original building to see Rothschild's initials encircling the top of the building facing State Street. Today, it is part of a complex and bustling university campus. This A.M. Rothschild building sometimes gets confused with the "other" Maurice L. Rothschild fine clothing store at 300 South State Street, at the corner of Jackson and State Streets. Maurice L. Rothschild was a cousin to the Rothschild's banking family that originated in France in the 1800s. Rothschild's Clothing Store was built by Holabird and Roche in 1906 and was a prime example of the Chicago School style of architecture. The clothing store closed in 1979 and

Following pages: State Street, Chicago, 1958. The New Year's crowd at the corner of State and Randolph Streets. Celebrants pack the street in front of Marshall Field's. *Courtesy of* Chicago Sun-Times *Newspaper Media/Archival Department.*

was purchased by the John Marshall Law School from Rothschild Properties, Inc. The school took up several floors of the twelve-story building for classrooms and offices, as well as space for an extensive library. Walgreens Drugstore occupies the basement and first floor today.

People and buildings have come and gone. At the northeast corner of State and Lake Streets, at 201 North State Street, was the famous iconic restaurant Fritzel's. Mike Fritzel operated the legendary restaurant from 1947 to 1972. There was no competing with the fine quality of foods Fritzel's served. Each order was individually prepared, cooked and properly served. The piano bar was famous for its cocktails. The restaurant had an extensive wine cellar and was considered one of the most frequented watering holes by the political and social elite, as well as visiting Hollywood celebrities. The three-martini lunch had a long history. Unfortunately, Fritzel's doors were closed in 1972.

Above: The new Sears at the northwest corner of State and Madison Streets, located in the old Boston Store building. Prior to becoming Sears, Walgreens was doing business at this same location. *Photo* © *Robert P. Ledermann.*

Opposite: Peacock Jewelers at Monroe and State Streets, with its impressive Roman numeral bronze clock and majestic peacock on top, was part of the original Palmer House complex in 1927. *Photo* © *Robert P. Ledermann.*

One of the famed Peacock entrance doors. Although the jewelry store is no longer there, the impressive door remains. *Photo © Robert P. Ledermann.*

The Boston Store is another building that was constructed in phases, from its beginning in 1905 through its final completion in 1917. It was quite a store back then. The Boston Store, at 22 West Madison at State Street, was built by Holabird and Roche. It was one unique building. In addition to its seventeen stories, it included a post office, a Western Union office, a savings bank, a barbershop, a first aid station and restaurants. A unique feature was the observation tower, some 325 feet above street level. And most interesting, a cigar factory on the seventeenth floor produced close to three million cigars a year. Rumors were that there was a tennis court for the employees up on the roof as well.

In the book *Give the Lady What She Wants* by Lloyd Wendt and Herman Kogan, there is a simple rhyme that children would sing: "All of the girls who wear high heels, they trade down at Marshall Field's. All the girls who scrub the floor, they trade at the Boston Store." The business was declining and closed in July 1948. The Walgreens Drugstore chain occupied the basement and first floors until 2001, when the building underwent a complete renovation. Sears again retails on State Street after many years of absence. In the lobby of this new Sears location, you can find mounted on the wall the original nameplate from 1932 that was on the exterior of the flagship building at State and Van Buren Streets.

On the southeast corner of Monroe and State Streets were the majestic doors to the C.D. Peacock jewelry store. It's founder, Elijah Peacock, started his business in 1877 and claimed to be Chicago's oldest jeweler. Walking into either the Liebolt's or Peacock's jewelry stores was a completely elegant experience. Only the finest jewelry and gifts were lavishly displayed, tempting you to buy some little bobble for yourself or a gift for a family member. Perhaps the merchandise wasn't in your price range, but it sure was fun looking, and the sales clerks didn't seem to mind showing off the quality pieces. In 1990, Peacock sold the business to the Gordon Jewelry Corporation and shortly thereafter left State Street.

THE FAIR/MONTGOMERY WARD

The Fair store was owned by Ernest J. Lehmann, who started a jewelry business on Clark Street. He was born in Tetrow, Mecklenburg-Schwerin, Germany, in 1849, came with his parents to America in 1858 and later settled in Chicago. His jewelry business was making a profit, and Lehmann wanted to expand his business. He acquired the land on Adams Street, between State and Dearborn. This is another building that had many names associated with it. Construction of the building, called "The Fair," replaced two smaller commercial buildings. Lehmann's new store, designed by William Le Baron Jenney and William Mundie, had twelve stories, with the construction of each section completed to his strict specifications. When it was completed in 1897, the store was of steel construction, with all the modern amenities shoppers were demanding. He had a Westinghouse electric lighting system, passenger and freight elevators and a fire safety system. He called his store "The Fair" because he believed "the store was like a fair because it offered many different things for sale and a cheap price." His customers found low-priced goods at alternative prices to the high-end, upscale items sold by other department stores.

Otto Young had a 50 percent interest in Lehmann's business. Young was born in Eberfield, Germany. He came to New York first and then moved to Chicago. He made a living by selling cigars to the wealthy guests in New York hotels. He, too, took a good look at the potential financial opportunities Chicago offered after the tragic fire of 1871. He came to Chicago with his wife and established Otto Young and Co., sellers of wholesale jewelry. He invested the jewelry profits into Chicago real estate and land. As a side note, the fire had affected him profoundly. In later years, he made sure that his summer home, Youngland Manor on the eastern shores of Lake Geneva, Wisconsin, was completely fireproof. (He lived during the winter season at 2032 South Calumet, next to Prairie Avenue.) This Italian-style summer palace was designed by Henry Lord Gay, and Richard Soutar was the contractor. The base cost was set at $150,000, but by the time all the elaborations had been added—including parquet flooring, hand-carved ceilings and gigantic

A postcard of Youngland (also known by many as Stone Manor), the summer home of Otto Young, located in Lake Geneva, Wisconsin. This vintage estate can be seen from the shoreline of Lake Geneva without having to take a boat. *Robert P. Ledermann, private collection.*

rooms—the total cost exceeded over $1 million. At the time, it was the highest-priced private home built on the lake.

Affectionately, Youngland was also called Stone Manor. This still existing mansion, when originally built, had over fifty rooms. In 1899, construction first began on the manor, and it took until May 1901 to be completed. If you ever travel to see it, look carefully at the façade to find the circles embedded into the marble depicting the faces of his four daughters: Cecilia, Catherine, Daisy and Laura. Young only lived to enjoy his summer home on the lake for a few short years, until his death in 1906. The names of his pallbearers read like a who's who in Chicago's history; Charles Wacker, A.C. Bartlett, Sam Allerton, R.T. Crane, Martin Ryerson and N.W Harris were among them. Today, Youngland/Stone Manor has been divided into six luxury condominiums.

As The Fair grew, so did its location. It occupied every building along the north side of Adams Street, between State and Dearborn. Lehmann's policy was to sell for less than the going price, but with smaller profits and a higher markup for sales in volume and bulk. Unfortunately, as the business profited, Lehmann's health suddenly worsened. He gave legal authority of the business to his wife, Augusta. Rumors indicate that he was committed to a mental institution until his death in

1900. I am sure the pressures of running a business and gaining a massive fortune attributed to his illness. Mrs. Lehmann became the sole owner of the store when she bought out her husband's partner, Otto Young. In 1925, she sold The Fair Store to the S.S. Kresge Company (later Kmart). She said of the sale, "I was tired and unable to give the business the attention it deserves." In 1957, retailing giant Montgomery Ward and Company purchased the State Street flagship store from Kresge.

At first, Wards retained The Fair name, as Kresge's had done. Then it was decided that a major remodeling of the seventy-four-year-old building was in order. The remodeling took some two years. In the 1940s and '50s, the store's toy department was called "The Toyfair." It had a functional, scaled-down model of the B&O Railroad that offered rides to customers.

I'll never forget, on a day late in August 1950, my sister took me down to The Fair to see Bobby Benson, the radio cowboy/child star, in the auditorium. He was promoting a line of cowboy western–style clothing, as well as his radio show, *Bobby Benson & the B-Bar-B Riders*.

The founder of the Ward family was Aaron Montgomery Ward, born in Chatham, New York, in 1844. As a young man, he also briefly worked for Marshall Field. Ward was known as the "Watchdog of the Lakefront" and later as a successful businessman. Chicago can thank Montgomery Ward for its beautiful lakefront. He fought the land developers who wanted to build along the lakefront. The only building he permitted was that of the Art Institute of Chicago. He spent his family's money constantly blocking new building proposals up and down the lakefront. He was quoted as saying, "I think there is not another man in Chicago who would have spent the money I have spent in this fight. I fought for the poor people of Chicago, not the millionaires." Ward made his fortune starting mail order catalogues in Chicago.

In 1936, Wards employee Robert L. May created the character and wrote the story for "Rudolph the Red-Nosed Reindeer." It was printed in 1939 and was given to 2.4 million children. It was reprinted again in 1946, with another 3.6 million copies distributed. Since then, to the delight of children throughout the world, merchandise of all kinds representing Rudolph has been manufactured. And the storybook about the little reindeer helping Santa has endured. The Robert L. May family donated all of his papers to his alumni college, Dartmouth.

Aaron Montgomery Ward died in 1913 at age sixty-nine, the victim of pulmonary edema, and is buried in the Rosehill Cemetery on Chicago's north side. The majority of his estate was given to Northwestern University and his adopted daughter. The store itself was valued as a real estate parcel and no longer the historical retail store of the past. Plans to close Wards on State Street were announced by its parent company (Mobile Corporation) in the newspapers in January 1984. The store was demolished that following April. The location stayed vacant until 2001, when construction began on a thirty-nine-story building for mixed-use retail and office space.

SEARS AND ROEBUCK

Richard Warren Sears acknowledged that mail order/catalogue business was key to his future as well. Successful merchants Aaron Montgomery Ward and Sears and Roebuck relied heavily on the Chicago Post Office to deliver their catalogues and magazine advertisements to their customers. With the establishment of the Parcel Post in 1913, these markets, along with the government, played an indispensible role in the expansion of Chicago's economy. These two businesses saw their catalogue/mail orders expand into vast sums of money and beyond when airmail service between New York and Chicago began in 1918.

Richard Warren Sears was born on December 7, 1863, in Stewartville, Minnesota, and at a young age entered the workforce to help supplement the family income after his father, James Warren, lost a considerable amount of money in a stock/farm deal. The story goes that while working at the North Redwood station for the Minneapolis & St. Louis Railroad, Sears received an offer from the manufacturers to sell a shipment of pocket watches that had been refused by a local merchant and left at the station. He quickly sold them to nearby farmers and passengers and was convinced that more money was to be made in a big city like Chicago. This was the career-changing experience he needed. He moved first to Minneapolis and established the R.S. Sears Watch Company. The next year, he set up headquarters in Chicago, near Dearborn and Randolph Streets. He hired a watchmaker and jewelry repairman from Indiana, Alvah Roebuck, who soon became his friend and partner. He opened another branch office in Toronto and implemented his first mail order business. Catalogue sales in 1893 were at first limited mainly to watches. Then Sears began to add other merchandise, from silverware, revolvers, baby carriages, bicycles, athletic equipment and even ready-to-assemble houses. These catalogues prospered due to high-quality goods and personal service. By 1894, the catalogue had grown to a hefty five hundred pages and was as much a part of the American household as the Bible.

In 1932, when the company moved into the flagship store at 401 South State Street at Van Buren, designed by William Le Baron Jenney in 1891, annual sales were tremendous. Sears and Roebuck introduced the Kenmore brand of appliances. It remained one of America's leading retailers. People had jumped on board, recognizing the potential growth of the company, and purchased common stock in the firm in 1906. Even back then, Sears and Roebuck had nine thousand employees throughout the country in mail order branches and stores from Dallas to Seattle, and by 1929, it had over three hundred stores. Much of Sears' success was due to a financial backer, Julius Rosenwald, who lived in the Kenwood neighborhood of Chicago. Rosenwald became a partner in the company in 1895 and then its president and chief executive after Richard Sears retired in 1909. As a side note, the radio station WLS was started by Sears Roebuck and Company in 1924. It was the pride of the store. The initials stood for "World's Largest Store."

During the 1980s and '90s, Sears slowly stopped issuing its big catalogues. The flagship store was progressing and thriving, along with the Hillman's food store in the basement, with all its fabulous specialties. I can remember all the smoked hams hanging up on stainless steel hooks against the white ceramic tiles surrounding the meat counter. Julius Rosenwald had supplied Sears and Roebuck with much of its clothing line. He was a huge clothing manufacturer and philanthropist. He donated millions and was the founder of the Chicago Museum of Science and Industry (formerly called the Rosenwald Museum), where he was president from 1927 to 1932. Sears remained on State Street until late 1983, when the Anvan Realty & Management Co., for an undisclosed price, renovated and reopened the building as an office complex that included the Robert Morris College.

MANDEL BROTHERS/WIEBOLDT'S

The immigrant family of Simon Klein had a business in 1855. Klein was the head of the family and uncle to brothers Solomon, Leon and Emanuel Mandel. He helped sponsor the brothers in their first store, which was located on Clark Street in 1865. By 1880, they had moved to One North State Street and employed eight hundred people. The store was rebuilt into a modern structure in 1912 by Holabird and Roche and again renovated in 1948.

Leon Mandel was at first reluctant to continue. Marshall Field owned the land where the business stood. Leon wanted to relocate to Michigan Avenue. The two businessmen settled their differences, and Field convinced Leon to stay by permitting Mandel to sign a ninety-nine-year lease. The Mandel Brothers Department Store geared its sales primarily toward the working-class family.

In the late 1800s, a second generation of Mandels continued with the firm. Annual sales surpassed any in the store's history, and then—like for any business during the Great Depression—profits slumped. Sales were dropping, but as fate would have it, the financial situation improved and profit margins again surged during World War II. Mandel Brothers also contributed to the war effort by donating three hundred air conditioners and other war products and needed supplies. Store executives, as well as employees, actively supported the local war bond drives. Founder Leon Mandel's son, Frederick Leon, temporarily left the business to serve in the Army Air Force. A branch of the WAC (Women's Army Corps) also had its location at the store.

After the war, the company planned to put $2.2 million into upgrades to the building. These were all deferred due to wartime restrictions. A new cafeteria, air conditioning, new escalators, a new communications system and electrical upgrades were finally completed in 1948.

More and more Chicagoans moved to the suburbs and stopped traveling to State Street to shop. With losses mounting and several Mandel family members over sixty, they began to think of selling or liquidating the business. Finally, after much family discussion and approval by the shareholders of both companies, Wieboldt's agreed to purchase Mandel Brothers for $2.75 million and various stock transfers. Wieboldt's acquired Mandel Brothers on State Street after a brief cleanup in 1960–61. Wieboldt's occupied the flagship store until 1987.

The founder of Wieboldt's retail family was born in Cuxhaven, Germany, in 1857. William A. Wieboldt's father passed away when William was only two. He was born into farm life, and the farm work was his informal schooling, making him an adult before his time. He was prompted by his uncle W.R. Wieboldt to come to America to work for him. For over two years, he did what his uncle asked of him, working in various retail positions in his uncle's stores. He found a bride, Anna Louisa Kruger, in 1883, and together, with only $2,600 in savings, they opened up their own store in the Chicago neighborhood of Grand and Ashland Avenues. They were happy and lived in a small flat above the store. A second store, opened in 1910, was in another neighborhood, on Milwaukee Avenue at Paulina.

Back at the flagship store, with remodeling completed, the shoppers appreciated the store and the moderately priced merchandise available. Wieboldt's was synonymous with S&H (Speery and Hutchinson) Green Stamps. Various retail stores and other businesses offered these stamps as a promotional thank you to customers for shopping with them. The customers, in turn, would paste the stamps in supplied blank books until the pages were filled and then redeem them for household items. Wieboldt's had these gift redemption centers located in most of its stores. It was a win-win situation and also good for business. Who couldn't use a free new kitchen appliance or a new bicycle for their kid? Wieboldt's toy department was fantastic. It was called "The Toyteria." In 1950, a sturdy, hardwood sixteen- by thirty-six-inch wagon with rubber wheels cost $9.98.

At Christmastime, Santa passed out Cinnamon Bear Silver Stars to top off your Christmas tree. This was all part of the Cinnamon Bear Christmas character that promoted Wieboldt's during the holidays. The Cinnamon Bear was a little brown bear cub with a green bow tie that took children Judy and Jimmy Barton on a trip to Maybeland in search of a silver star to place on their own Christmas tree. The Cinnamon Bear radio program originated in Hollywood, California, and consisted of twenty-six episodes heard on radios across the country every holiday season. The program encouraged children's imaginations to take them to places they could only dream of. Visits to the candy pirates, the singing forest and a root beer ocean were some of the fantastic destinations they would hear about. There was a television program as well, where Patty-O-Cinnamon, a playful puppet, would act out the stories. In those days, with the Cinnamon Bear, Uncle Mistletoe and Rudolph the Red-Nosed Reindeer, it was great to be a kid.

Wieboldt's bargain basement had exactly what you didn't need at a bargain price, so even though you didn't need something, you purchased it anyway and felt proud about saving money. I can still remember that the basement had a full-service shoe repair and a snack shop with delicious malted milks. It also had access to the State Street subway. My wife enjoyed shopping in the ladies' department on the first floor for her Ship-In-Store cotton blouses and in the hat department for her Easter bonnet.

Wieboldt's had two fine restaurants called the Travertine Room, decorated in turquoise blue, beiges and gold, and the Wabash Grill, which was usually frequented by businessmen. William Werner Wieboldt's son succeeded him as company president when he retired in 1923. The store flourished for more than sixty good years, even through hard times, until 1986, when Wieboldt's had trouble making a profit and was forced into bankruptcy, from which it never recovered. The remaining stores were also financially drained and closed. William A. Wieboldt passed away in 1954 at age ninety-seven, after a full and memorable life in retail.

THE STATE STREET MALL

Under Mayor Jane Byrne and city officials, it was decided in 1974 that the city needed more glamour. The federal government also recommended that Chicago's air be cleaner. Mall project manager Robert French of the City Bureau of Archives said:

> *The mall is there to be seen and used, but what we did is a major construction to the street's environment. Private cars are gone and so are a lot of exhaust fumes. Those old buses' boarding ramps in the middle of the street are gone. Drainage will be better. Sidewalks are wider, and there will be escalators and elevated tracks and shelters for the bus riders. It was a mess—a lot of the wire and pipes have to be charted, but the files were spread all over the city. One wrong move and we would have blacked out one half of the Loop area. The place needs a fresh look. It took twice as long to walk the street as to take a bus or taxi cab—something had to give. Terrible congestion.*

Jerome Butler, an architect for the city, drew up the plans for the new mall, along with Kiycki Kikuchi. Construction started in 1978 and was completed in 1979. Andy Knott, in a *Tribune* article, noted:

> *Another wrong move and we might have had a gas explosion. It was just a matter of luck that the project did not run into any problems. We all were on call 24 hours a day and the contractor was very careful throughout construction. We all did our homework too.*

On Monday, October 29, 1979, at the mall's official opening, Chicagoans saw a 20- by 440-foot island at its northern start: Wacker Drive and State Street. It was covered with freshly sodden grass and lined with benches. Planters containing Linden and Honey Locust trees completed the mini park's appearance. A sidewalk of black hexagonal asphalt and granite blocks extend from the storefront to the new speckled-granite curbs at the street. Sixteen escalators were spaced along the mall's nine blocks, to be used to move CTA (Chicago Transportation Authority) riders from the subway to street level or from street level to the elevated train platforms. There were also new stairwells for the same purpose and two enclosed bus shelters per block, as well as thirty-two multi-use kiosk booths for newspaper stands, postage stamp machines, telephones and dispensing information to pedestrians. Approximately 125 planters, each 8 feet in diameter and containing either more Linden trees or other greenery—including junipers, evergreens and flowers—graced the mall and were watered by automatic sprinklers. A second, smaller island at Congress and State Streets complemented the main one with similar greenery. As lovely as this was, it wasn't to be long-lived; the traffic was back on State Street in 1996 under

Mayor Richard M. Daley.

The city, along with the Greater State Street Council working with the participating stores, had a "People Week" in the 1960s. In the 1980s, it would be called "State Street Days." The street was open to vendors, painters and artists, and the public could stroll from one end of State Street to the other and purchase unique gifts.

The unforgettable dime stores and drug and candy shops included Woolworths, S.S. Kresge, Walgreens, Fanny May, De Mets and the fantastic Krantz Candies. Each of these places had its very own personality. The intoxicating fragrance of fresh chocolates enticed you to purchase a pound of fudge. The memory of the sound of the creaking wooden floors when walking into the dime stores, where you would look at all the wonderful items on the waist-high counters, is a fond one.

Dime stores. Just saying the words in my mind brings a smile to my lips. Going to a dime store to spend your allowance on a toy you wanted was enjoyable. It is so sad that in today's digital society, our children will never experience the sheer joy of having a few coins in their pocket and spending them at a dime store. The F.W. Woolworth (Franklin Winfield Woolworth) and S.S. Kresge dime stores were two of these memorable institutions.

Did you need a Turkish towel, men's shirt collars, shoe polish, dress shields, wash buckets, a carpet sweeper, a wood curtain stretcher, a rug beater, women's snuggies, aluminum coffee percolators, a tea cozy, a double boiler, hair pins, mustache wax or oil cloth? Kresge's and Woolworths had all these items and more; they were somewhat like the dollar stores of today. Sure, you could purchase a coloring book or a hair net, but could you buy lead or rubber toy soldiers or two yards of pink polka dot ribbon? Indeed you could at the special places on State Street, the dime stores with their little metal space dividers on the counters separating the merchandise into prices: ten cents, ninety cents or even as much as $1.98. It was interesting to stop in frequently to see all the new items on sale that hadn't been there the last time.

Most dime stores had soda fountains and luncheonette areas. These had counters, usually against a wall, with stools surrounding them and perhaps a few booths to sit down with friends or family. Ice cream tasted like ice cream back then—rich, creamy and fresh. Your average ice cream sundae was thirty-five cents. Many Chicagoans have wonderful memories of the dime stores on State Street, up and down the block.

Sebastian Spering Kresge was born in 1867 to a very frugal Swiss farmer. Working as a traveling salesman, he managed to save $8,000. He partnered with John McCrory and opened his first stores in Memphis, Tennessee, and Detroit, Michigan, in 1899. He was the success he set out to be. He allegedly said, "I think I was successful because I saved and because I heeded good advice. I worked and I didn't work only eight hours a day, but sometime eighteen hours. When one starts at the bottom and learns to scrape, then everything becomes easy." Unfortunately, his private life wasn't so joyful. He married three times. He stayed with his third wife, Clara Swaine, until his death in 1966. Despite his thriftiness, he was a respected employer and philanthropist. He offered his employees profit sharing, bonuses, sick leave, pensions and paid holidays, and through the Kresge Foundation, he gave millions away.

Franklin Winfield Woolworth, coincidentally, was also the son of a (potato) farmer. He was born in New York in 1852 and worked in a general store as a stock boy. He noticed that leftover merchandise was not selling unless it was placed on a separate table with a reduced price. He left his employer and went into business with his brother, Charles Sumner Woolworth. Surprisingly, his first store was a disaster. The F.W Woolworth Company was incorporated in 1911 and began to open five- and ten-cent stores. Franklin married Jennie Creighton, and they had three daughters. Sadly, one of them, Edna, committed suicide. Years later, Barbara Hutton, a granddaughter, became a Hollywood movie star. Franklin had the famous Woolworth Building in New York City built in 1913, when he was sixty-one.

Woolworth, through contacts in Europe—especially England and Germany—imported and introduced beautiful, shiny, hand-made glass Christmas ornaments into all his dime stores. They were most welcomed and, at prices people could afford, made the holidays brighter as well. Whatever you needed, it could be found at these dime stores. Throughout the year, holidays or special days would come up, and

A 1911 postcard of the interior of Kranz's candy store on State Street across from Marshall Field's. The original taffy cutter (chopping axe, inset opposite) was 5.25 inches long, allowing the clerk to chop off a section of toffee or peanut brittle. John Kranz was a German confectioner who opened the State Street store in 1881 at 126–132 North State, one of Chicago's best-known candy stores. The house specialties, besides its ice cream, were the chocolate sodas. No food was served. It's lyrical art nouveau interior, with bisque marble pillars and Mexican onyx tables, was decorated by R.W. Bates of Boston and Abner Crossman of Chicago. Some of the store's regulars were Kate Buckingham and Mrs. John T. Pirie. Kranz went out of business in 1947. *Robert P. Ledermann, private collection.*

you could do one-stop shopping at a State Street Kresge's or Woolworth dime store. From a toy or live parakeet for a child's birthday present, complete with wrapping paper and a birthday card, to an American flag for the Fourth of July, a Halloween face mask or a complete set of dishes for a bride-to-be, everything was for sale at the dime stores on State Street.

Charles Walgreen was born in the area of Galesburg, Illinois, in 1873, the son of Swedish immigrants. In 1897, he passed the Illinois State Board of Pharmacy test and enlisted in the Illinois National Guard, doing pharmaceutical chores. Afterward, with a small loan from his father, he opened his first small drugstore at 4134 South Cottage Grove in 1901. He sold typical health-related products, such as bar soap, tooth powders, toiletries, tonics, perfumes, shaving equipment, shoe polish, pills, cough syrup and tablets for various ailments of the head and stomach. His idea of letting customers call and place an order for his clerks to deliver was a big hit and made his business even more successful. He added soda fountains that included hot lunches. One Walgreens store on State Street was at Randolph and another was at Madison. Today, the only Walgreens store remaining on State Street is at State and Jackson. It was written that the chocolate malted milkshake was invented after one of his employees added vanilla ice cream to the plain malted drink using only milk. By 1926, Walgreens had acquired ninety-two store locations in the Chicago area. Walgreens developed from a neighborhood store into the nation's largest drugstore chain. For years, Walgreen and his family lived in a beautiful mansion at 116th Street and Longwood Drive in the Morgan Park neighborhood until his passing in 1939 at age sixty-six.

The smaller shops up and down State Street are not to be overlooked. They, too, have interesting histories, as do the banking firms that dotted the street, changing names over the years or completely folding.

Henry C. Lytton opened his fine clothing store at State and Jackson Streets in 1887. He named it, affectionately, "The Hub," calling attention to its central location and the store's slogan of the "World's Greatest Clothing Store." He thought that by thinking big and saying so, he would succeed. His promotions for the store were attention grabbing to say the least. Lytton used the local newspaper heavily to advertise his promotions. One time, he tossed free overcoats off the roof of the store to the crowds gathered below. He hired only the best employees, who were particularly courteous and approached each customer with friendly voices, always

One of the posters seen surrounding the walls of the soda fountain at Woolworths. *Robert P. Ledermann, private collection.*

dressed accordingly in the "Lytton Look." At Christmastime, all the male clerks were required to wear the red wool vests management gave them as gifts.

Henry Lytton retired and turned the business over to his son, George, only to return and serve as president when his son died in 1933. In 1946, in honor of Mr. Lytton's 100th birthday, the name of the store was officially changed to Lytton's. Mr. Lytton remained president until his death in 1949 at the amazing old age of 103. For the next 35 years or so, Lytton's remained on State Street, until a bankruptcy judgment forced the store to close in 1986.

We mostly remember all the smaller restaurants and shops—stores like Bonds, Benson/Rixon, Baskins, Stevens, the Lerner Shop, Evans Furs, Richmond Brothers and even Shoppers Corner and Smokey Joes. What an array of unique and different businesses State Street has hosted over the years! Now all have gone.

One brick at a time...

7

STATE STREET TODAY

Block 37 is located at the heart of State Street, surrounded by four major streets: Randolph, Dearborn, Washington and State. Prior to its revitalization and renaming, the grid of streets had office buildings, supermarkets, shoe stores, retail clothing stores and the great United Artist and Roosevelt Theaters. Chicagoans were not coming back into the city after the great suburban migration, and these businesses suffered neglect, deterioration and financial decline.

The city elected to totally demolish and level all the buildings in this square-block area in 1989. Unfortunately, various financial problems with potential developers stalled the project and left the land vacant for the next two decades. Years passed, and still the plans were in limbo. Finally, under the direction of Chicago's (former) first lady, Maggie Daley, working with the city, it was recognized that this area could be put to good use, other than just being an eyesore to visitors and Chicagoans. It was fenced in and boarded up. Pigeons inhabited it, and an occasional homeless person called it home. Daley elected to change this. She dubbed the area "Block 37," referring to the original fifty-eight city blocks established in the 1800s. The only original structure left standing was the active Commonwealth Edison transformer building, which still supplies and distributes power to that area of the city.

Daley created a beautiful park-like oasis for use in the spring and summer, and turned the area into an ice-skating ring, sponsored by the park district, in the winter. It was a warm and welcomed sight. She sponsored and oversaw an after-school art project, "Gallery 37." Students of Chicago schools interested in the arts created works of art and displayed their projects under huge white tents in Block 37. Strolling through the pavement paths and viewing the artwork by gifted young people was inspiring. This sheltered, pleasant area lasted for years, until finally, the first financially

supported construction started in earnest in May 2007. Today, Block 37 is a mixed-use structure that includes the new WBBM Channel 2/Chicago CBS studios. It shares the street with the ABC Chicago Channel 7 television studio in the old State and Lake Theater at 190 North State. The underground repairs to the "pedway" and subway connections on State Street reopened as well. As of this printing, Block 37 is not financially stable. Its developer, Joseph Freed and Associates, lost control and is involved in court proceedings with the Bank of America Corporation, which is filing a foreclosure suit.

With the renewed and revitalized interest of the universities in the empty, bigger buildings up and down State Street, Chicago has experienced a breath of fresh air. The "campus" was created at the south end of State Street and comprises mainly schools of higher learning: DePaul University, the School of the Art Institute, Robert Morris College, the John Marshall Law School, Roosevelt University and Colombia College, to mention a few. Student dorms dot the area, housing the campus's students. The old Goldblatt's building now is the DePaul Center, with a Barnes & Noble Bookstore on the first floor. The Robert Morris College is in the old Sears building at State and Van Buren Streets. The John Marshall Law School is in the old Maurice L. Rothschild clothing building at State and Jackson Streets, with the Walgreens Drugstore on the first floor. The School of the Art Institute currently occupies several floors of the Sullivan Center (formerly the old Carson, Pirie Scott Building), as well as other learning locations). Roosevelt University is in the old Auditorium Building on Michigan Avenue. Columbia College is in the (old) New World Building, next to Orchestra Hall on Michigan Avenue.

Right: The corner of State and Randolph Streets, with the final work being completed on Block 37. *Photo © Robert P. Ledermann.*

Opposite: The beginning of Block 37 at ground level, circa 1990s. In the foreground is State Street, to the left is Washington, crossing over is Dearborn and to the right is Randolph (not seen). This picture was taken from Macy's Walnut Room Restaurant on the seventh floor. The Daley Plaza can be seen across the block, with city hall, home to Chicago's mayors, on the fifth floor. *Photo © Robert P. Ledermann.*

It is interesting to note that the *Chicago Sun-Times* newspaper printed an article on February 25, 2011, written by staff reporter David Roeder and Art Golab, entitled "New Life in the Loop." The article indicated that "the 65,500 students downtown spend more than $60 million annually shopping and eating" and that "the Loop contains 3.3 million square feet of retail space, with annual sales topping $2 billion." The writers' sources were the Chicago Loop Alliance and Goodman Williams Group Real Estate Research.

The revitalization of the Theater District in the Loop included a cluster of Broadway-type theaters: the Cadillac Palace, the Oriental Theatre, the Bank of America Theatre in the old Shubert Theatre and, around the corner, the Goodman Theatre (formerly the Michael Todd Theatre). All underwent restorations that brought back their original elegance.

The Palmer House Hilton hotel was beautifully restored from 2007 to 2009 at a cost of over $170 million, with a total of 1,639 guest rooms. The renovations to its original grand elegance are breathtaking. Every minute detail was attended to in order to restore the "Grand Lady of State Street."

The famous Empire Room (once known as one of Chicago's best supper nightclubs) in the Palmer House. The impressive stairway is flanked by winged golden angels, each covered in a layer of twenty-four-carat gold. Each angel weighs approximately two tons, and both were designed by Lewis Comfort Tiffany. These were the largest sculptures Tiffany created. *Photo © Robert P. Ledermann.*

The Reliance Building, now Hotel Burnham on North State Street, completed a wonderful restoration in 2006. It painstakingly preserved the massive plate glass windows that were one of the features of the original skyscraper. Today, the lobby on the first floor shares space with its signature restaurant, the Atwood, named after designer Charles B. Atwood of the Daniel H. Burnham architectural firm. In 1970, it was listed on the National Register of Historic Places, and it was designated a National Historical Landmark in 1976.

This growth in the arts, culture and schooling has helped tourism come back to Chicago. There is a new vitality to the hotel guests that attend Broadway-in-Chicago performances. All of this interest in the rebirth of Chicago nightlife is beneficial for Chicago's future.

Newer or established neighbors continue adding to the tapestry of the street. The Gene Siskel Film Center at 164 North State Street is part of the School of the Art Institute of Chicago and is dedicated to presenting the best in independent and world cinema.

The corner of State and Randolph Streets, looking up at the Joffrey Ballet Studios, located across from Macy's (formerly Marshall Field's). *Photo © Robert P. Ledermann.*

The Mo Mo Building, which welcomed the Joffrey Ballet Studios at Randolph and State Streets, has been a fantastic addition to the arts on State.

There have been playful experiences for Chicagoans over the years, too. In 1999, Chicago had the cows. Life-sized bovine beauties appeared on the streets of Chicago. State Street had its share of these painted and decorated cows created by Chicago artists, architects, photographers and designers. The idea was originally thought of by Beat Seeberger and was first presented in the city of Zurich, Switzerland. Then, Chicago had "Suite Home Chicago" in 2001, when oversized pieces of outdoor furniture, couches, loveseats and chairs were painted, decorated and scattered about Chicago.

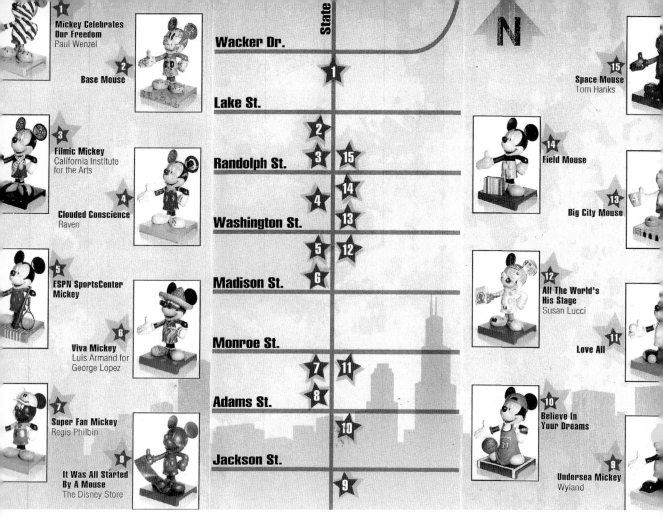

The Mickey Mouse chart indicating where the statues were located up and down State Street from Wacker Drive to Jackson. *Robert P. Ledermann, private collection.*

In 2004, Chicago saw a collection of six-foot statues of Mickey Mouse for the seventy-fifth anniversary of the Mickey Mouse character. In Chicago, this event was cosponsored by Disney and the Greater State Street Council (now the Chicago Loop Alliance). Each Mickey weighed up to seven hundred pounds and was constructed of polyurethane and steel. Each statue had a star or famous artist who had inspired the statue's design and chose the charity to which the monies from the statue's sale would go. Regis Philbin had *Super Fan*, which portrayed Mickey as a golfer wearing Notre Dame's colors. Tom Hanks had *Space Mouse*. The California Institute for the Arts inspired *Filmic Mickey*, and Brian Matson inspired one with Marshall Field's colors called *Field Mouse*. They were scattered along State Street from Wacker Drive to Jackson Street.

All of the statues came from California and were sent to various cities. Walt Disney was born in Chicago, so Chicago was the first city to host an exhibit, with fifteen of the seventy-five statues.

In 2010, Chicago was being watched. The city had a thirty-foot eyeball staring at it, complete with blood vessels and a huge blue iris. Tasset's *Eye* sculpture was made of fiberglass and was painted by hand.

These and other fun ideas to attract tourism were all sponsored by the Chicago Loop Alliance (formerly the Greater State Street Council) in connection with various groups. The Chicago Loop Alliance has been a vanguard in the city, always watching and continuing to be part of making Chicago's history.

Our South State Street anchor is the Chicago Public Library's Harold Washington Center. It's the largest center in the nation. It was built at a cost of $144 million. The 761,000-square-foot building houses approximately 1,625,000 books and 12,260 periodicals and serials. This world-class structure at Van Buren and

A Mickey Mouse statue located in front of the Marshall Field's store on State Street in 2004. *Photo © Robert P. Ledermann.*

State Streets captures the flavor of nineteenth-century architecture while featuring twentieth-century technology. The crowning touch of the library is the exquisite Winter Garden, where patrons can read under the skylight that rises 52 feet above branches and greenery. This majestic building was added to State Street's history in October 1991.

The older Chicago Public Library Building must thank our former first lady of Chicago, Maggie Daley, for saving it from the wrecking ball. She worked diligently with the city planners and financial backers to preserve its original grandeur, including the marvelous Tiffany Dome. It is called the Chicago Cultural Center, located on Michigan Avenue between Randolph and Washington. Thank goodness this wonderful building was saved and that Chicago doesn't stop repairing and correcting itself, one brick at a time. One brick at a time…

CLOSING REMARKS

Our concept of history is constantly changing. That is especially apparent when you go to State Street after not having been there for a while. You might hear someone say, "Wow, I didn't know that building was there" or "What happened to…" This could be the case for State Street at any given time of year, even today. People often say that "change is for the good" and that things become "new and improved." Although these remarks have some truth, they are not always accurate. Some people are uncomfortable with change, but in Chicago—and especially on State Street—it's all about change.

When the Picasso was unveiled in the Daly Plaza/Center in 1967, perhaps you were unsure whether you would accept it. There was so much criticism after its dedication. Chicagoans were suspicious and cautious at first. Would this modern sculpture fit in? Today, it is accepted as one of the highlights to be seen by visitors and Chicagoans alike. If anyone now were to question or petition for its removal, I dare say heads would roll. Can you even remember what was there before the Picasso appeared?

On the night of November 14, 1958, I was standing in the middle of State Street, along with thousands of other people, to watch the unveiling of the new brilliant light fixtures that arched out into the street. All the merchants had contributed to replace the old, obsolete lampposts from 1926. Today, they have again been replaced by reproductions of the old lampposts, but with a modern and stronger twist to conserve energy.

The line "what's old is new again" comes to mind. When I was a young boy, skinny, narrow ties were the fashion, and then those were out and the wider ties were in. Today, the ties are narrow again.

When asked by a newspaper reporter why he wore only double-breasted suits when they were out of style, (the late) Basil Rathbone replied that he wore them because he felt comfortable in them, and looked good in them, and not because it was the fashion of the day.

Years ago—and not that many—people didn't want records anymore. You could not sell a vinyl record for ten or fifteen cents. Today, surprisingly enough, records are coming back into popularity.

To me, there is nothing like holding a book in your hands. There is nothing wrong with the convenience of the new e-readers when at the beach or on a plane, but nothing is more heartwarming then a den, a home library or an office with a massive wooden bookcase overflowing with first editions with autographs.

It was my pleasure to work for (at that time) the world's largest bookstore, Kroch's & Brentano's. Kroch's & Brentano's was the bookstore to go to for any author who stopped in Chicago. Kroch's flagship store was at 29 South Wabash Avenue, and on the fourth floor were the executive offices. Upon entering the conference room, there was an immense bookcase that covered the entire wall, from floor to ceiling, filled with first edition, autographed books. Books from Ernest Hemmingway, Rogers & Hammerstein, Robert Frost, presidents as far back as Taft and movie stars, to name a few. It was impressive. There was a plaque on the wall with the words of one of my favorite sayings by Clarence Day entitled "The World of Books":

> *The world of books is the most remarkable creation of man: nothing else that he builds ever lasts. Monuments fall; nations perish; civilizations grow old and die out. After an era of darkness new races build another; but in the world of books are volumes that live on; still as young and fresh as the day they were written; still telling men's hearts of the hearts of men centuries dead.*

This quote sums up my feelings concerning books and is also relevant to State Street. The more things change, the more they remain the same—be it ties, books, buildings or bricks. One brick at a time…

BIBLIOGRAPHY

Benjamin, Susan, and Stuart Cohen. *Great Houses of Chicago*. New York: Acanthus Press, 2008.

Chicago Historical Society. *Chicago: Highlights of Its History*. Booklet, n.d.

Chicago Tribune. "Yesterday and Today." October 28, 1979.

Chicago Tribune staff. *Chicago Days: 150 Defining Moments in the Life of a Great City*. Edited by Stevenson Swanson. Chicago: Contemporary Books, 1997.

Dennis, John, Jr. "Marshall Field a Great Mercantile Genius." *Everybody's Magazine* 14, no. 3 (March 1906).

Donovan, Lisa. "Civil Leaders Seek To Honor Champion of Open Spaces." *Chicago Sun-Times*, August 1, 2010.

Field Glass, December 3, 1938.

Glibota, Ante, and Frederic Edelmann. *A Guide to 150 Years of Chicago Architecture*. Chicago: Chicago Review Press, 1985.

Greene, Joan. *A Chicago Tradition: Marshall Field's, Food and Fashion*. San Francisco: Pomegranate Press for Chicago Cultural Center Foundation, 2005.

Grossman, James R., Ann Durkin Keating and Janice L. Reiff. *The Encyclopedia of Chicago*. Chicago: University of Chicago Press, 2004.

Grossman, Ron. "Store of History." *Chicago Tribune*, June 12, 1988.

Hayner, Don, and Tom McNamee. *Metro Chicago Almanac*. Chicago: Bonus Books Inc., 1989.

Hoekstra, Dave. "Scrawls of Fame." *Chicago Sun-Times*, March 28, 2011, Show Case section.

Holton, Lisa. *For Members Only: A History and Guide to Chicago's Oldest Private Clubs*. Chicago: Lake Claremont Press, 2008.

Howard, T.J. "Window Treatment." *Eleven* (December 1989).

Hull, Hamilton. *Chicago and Marshall Field's 85th Year*. Souvenir booklet. Chicago: Marshall Field's, 1937.

Jones, Sandra M. "Bank of America Buys Block 37 For $100 Million." *Chicago Tribune*, March 24, 2011.

Kamin, Blair. "The Mystery of the Big Carson's Clock that Never Was." *Chicago Tribune*, March 22, 2011.

————. "Timeless State Street Will Be Less Interesting." *Chicago Tribune*, n.d.

Kimbraugh, Emily. *Through Charley's Door*. New York: Harper Brothers, 1952.

Marshall Field's. *Chicago and Marshall Field*. Booklet, 1937.

————. *Marshall Field's State Street Visitor's Guide*. Booklet, n.d.

Meeker, Arthur. *Prairie Avenue*. New York: Alfred A. Knopf, Inc., Boyoi Books, 1949.

Nickel, Richard, Aaron Siskind, John Vinci and Ward Miller. *The Complete Architecture of Adler and Sullivan*. N.p.: Published by the Richard Nickel Committee, 2010.

Pridmore, Jay. *Marshall Field's: A Building Book from the Chicago Architecture Foundation*. San Francisco: Pomegranate Press, 2002.

Rice, Charles B. *The Field Memorial Library, Conway, Mass.* Boston: Arakelyan Press, 1907.

Roeder, David, and Art Golabon. "New Life in the Loop, the Scoop on the Loop." *Chicago Sun-Times*, February 25, 2011.

Sawyers, June Skinner. *Chicago Portraits*. Chicago: Loyola Press, 1991.

Siegelman, Steve. *The Marshall Field's Cookbook.* Photography by Maren Caruso. San Francisco: Book Kitchen, 2006.

Siry, Joseph. *Carson, Pirie, Scott, Louis Sullivan and the Chicago Department Store*. Chicago: University of Chicago Press, 1988.

Skertic, Mark. "Chicago's Wealthiest Few Lived It Up in the Gilded Age." *Chicago Sun-Times*, November 8, 1999.

Sneed, Michael. "Monster Sale." *Chicago Sun-Times*, March 23, 2011.

Soucek, Gayle. *Marshall Field's: The Store that Helped Build Chicago*. Charleston, SC: The History Press, 2010.

Sullivan, Mary Elen. *Cows on Parade in Chicago*. Photography by Simon Koenig. Kreuzlingen, Switzerland: Neptun Art, 1999.

Sutcliffe, J.A., ed. *The Sayings of Winston Churchill*. London: Duckworth, 1992.

Tyre, William H. *Chicago's Historic Prairie Avenue*. Charleston, SC: Arcadia, 2008.

Wendt, Lloyd, and Herman Kogan. *Give the Lady What She Wants*. Chicago: Rand McNally, 1952.

Wilk, Deborah. *Suite Home Chicago: An International Exhibit of Urban Street Furniture by Ilka Michel*. Photography by Ilka Michel. Kreuzlingen, Switzerland: Neptun Verlog, 2001.

Wolfmeyer, Ann, and Mary Burns Gage. *Lake Geneva: Newport of the West*. Vol. 1. Lake Geneva, WI: Lake Geneva Historical Society, 1976.

ABOUT THE AUTHOR

Robert P. Ledermann was born and raised on the northwest side of Chicago. Working downtown throughout his adult life in the retail and credit fields, he appreciated and enjoyed Chicago and its history. The fine museums, libraries, restaurants and learning institutions all contributed to his love of research and writing. His fondness for the history of State Street, with all the fascinating people who added to its growth, encouraged Robert to write this book.

Robert is highly regarded as an expert on Marshall Field's and Uncle Mistletoe and is a huge Chicago and State Street nostalgia buff. His working history started at Lytton's and then Rothschild's. He was a member of the credit board for the Illinois Retail Merchants Association when he worked for the Kroch's & Brentano's Book Store for seventeen years as credit manager. He was a one-time member of the Greater State Street Council (now the Chicago Loop Alliance).

He has written numerous articles, given historical lectures and written two other books: *Chicago's State Christmas Parade* and *Christmas on State Street: 1940s and Beyond*.

He is currently enjoying retirement to the fullest and continues to be active in his neighborhood. His hobbies include collecting Chicago memorabilia.

Visit us at
www.historypress.net